Somewhere
between
Kindergarten
and God

Faye and Ron
Blessings to both
of you
♡

Lesta Bertoia

SOMEWHERE
BETWEEN
KINDERGARTEN
AND GOD

MINI-MEMOIRS
ABOUT THE
MUNDANE AND
THE MYSTICAL

LESTA BERTOIA

HAMPTON ROADS
PUBLISHING COMPANY, INC.

Cover design by Steve Amarillo
Cover photo by PhotoDisc and Nova Development Corp.

Hampton Roads Publishing Company, Inc.
1125 Stoney Ridge Road
Charlottesville, VA 22902

434-296-2772
fax: 434-296-5096
email: hrpc@hrpub.com
www.hrpub.com

If you are unable to order this book from your local
bookseller, you may order directly from the publisher.
Call 1-800-766-8009, toll-free.

Library of Congress Catalog Card Number: 2001094966
ISBN 1-57174-240-9

10 9 8 7 6 5 4 3 2 1

Printed on acid-free paper in Canada

Dedication

This book is dedicated to . . . so many people I don't know who to name first, because there is really no order of importance. I almost want to say, simply, to everybody in it, to all those on this side of the veil and on that side who have been my Reminders . . . and leave it at that. You know who you are, and what you have given me, and why I want to give what I can back to you.

But I do want some of you, at least, to see your names on this page.

So . . .

To the most enduringly patient, faithful, and enlightening members of my Light Being family, Eric and Fawni.

To my partner and inspiration, David.

To Val and Celia, Harry and Brigitta, Raine and Eli, Clark and Luke, and Nicole, for being the finest family and the most wonderful teachers of love I could have asked for.

To Marilyn, Brooke, Dick, John, Sue, and Bernard, for being the original catalysts and enthusiastic supporters of my writing this book.

To the grandchild whose name I will know soon.

To the angels, both human and winged, who have guided me.

To God-Goddess, the universe, Great Spirit, Great Mystery, the Source, the All, the One whose name cannot be pronounced any more than the orchestration of an infinitely uplifting symphony can be pronounced in a single word.

To every one of you who reads this book and is Reminded.

Contents

Preface

This book is either an act of God or an act of faith; I'm not sure which. I began writing it with no credentials whatsoever, a nobody presuming to be somebody with something to say, but the more I felt compelled to write about whatever came up during the year it was being written, the more that everything I had to say turned out to be a surprise.

I didn't remember until they all showed up in one place how many close encounters of the twelfth kind I'd been privileged to experience. I didn't plan on being a champion of self-sovereignty and mega-polarity, or, as a visitor to the planet, to extend my congratulations to humanity. I wasn't prepared to discover that within this year of my life a plot would unfold as if I'd intended its crescendo and conclusion. But, of course, I *did.* Intend it. And I didn't. For, as I've learned, I am, as you are, a vastly powerful and playful being who chose forgetfulness as the wrapping paper around an endlessly intriguing, mysterious present, one which constantly unfolds itself . . . into just what we imagined.

When I'd finished, I needed a title. I had chosen a format similar to Robert Fulghum's in *Everything I Need to Know I Learned in Kindergarten.* Although my chapters are loosely connected (since they happen sequentially over the course of a year), each chapter has a self-contained theme, often rounded off with a one-line observation. I had been inspired by the revelations shared among a group of friends who gathered to discuss Neale Donald Walsch's *Conversations with God.* (The belief that I could write a publishable book took root with their encouragement.) I had also come to discern an underlying premise that gave cohesion to my musings. Each of us is on our own path, somewhere between kindergarten and God, somewhere between the mundane and the mystical. As divine souls condensed into human bodies, we can only hope to achieve a working balance between this grounded reality and that ethereal one.

My balancing act was a challenge. At the same time that I was remembering the gifts given to me by a family of Light Beings, I was coping (rather poorly) with my partner's ex-girlfriend. In between experiencing life as a lucid dream and being guided by those on the Other Side, I was juggling menopause and a suicidal ex-husband. That I can astral-travel doesn't mean that my healing powers are anything more than accidental.

Arguments with God clarified some problems, but I had help, too, from a pair of faulty windshield wipers, a couple of ducks, and my two children, who remember their past lives. My flesh-and-blood teachers also included an old woman in neon green running shoes with the eye of an angel, a ten-year-old boy who levitates, and a man I met through the personals, whose ad on the Web included a photo of himself with two heads. How could I resist?

My assistants in the invisible realm have been, among others, my father, who died in 1978; my friend's deceased mother, who tossed a penny from heaven into my kitchen sink; a spirit wolf who helped me contact my sister; and several of my own selves, who appear to live in one dimension over, either this way or that. With their help I've explored such experiences and concepts as paradox, joy, universal energy, freedom, miracles, abortion, time, and bringing heaven to Earth.

I hope that by sharing both the pitfalls of my personal life and the iridescent visions whispered to me by the light of dawn, I will be reminding you of at least two things. The first is that even if one part of you is ricocheting off the walls of the maze in frustrating attempts to find a way out, another is sitting on top of the wall, clapping and giggling and pointing to the exit. And the second? Humanity's emergence from a long and bitter winter is as forthcoming as the arrival of a warm and welcome spring.

But after all, perhaps, together, we can conclude only one thing. That life is a mystery is the best thing about it.

1

Neon Green

In search of my lost soul, and tired of driving all night, I parked myself under a Tennessee rest-area tree with my journal propped on my lap and watched the rising sun bathe the sky in glory. A station wagon that looked to be about a thousand years old, sporting a spare tire and several odd suitcases on its rack, pulled up beside my van, steam cascading from under its rusty hood. It shuddered and rattled into silence. An old man with a long gray beard that hid his overalls' bib eased himself out from behind the steering wheel. Holding the stiff bend of his back with one hand, he slowly stretched himself upright. He pushed up his baseball cap, studied the steam, and decided to raise the hood. His wife, who'd emerged from the other side and done a quick little running-in-place warm-up, poked her fuzzy head in under the hood, too. Her strawberry-pink sweat pants were hiked up over the bulge of her stomach, revealing her crepe-paper ankles above her neon green running shoes. He shook his head thoughtfully. "'Pears to be overheatin'," he observed astutely.

She looked at him with unabashed admiration, nodded judiciously, and then noticed me sitting a few yards away. "You a man or a woman?" she directed at me as she approached.

I tugged my long skirt further down over my ankles and ran my fingers through my newly short-cropped hair, quite at a loss for words.

"Cain't hardly tell these days no more. You wouldn't be one o' them preachers, wouldja?"

I questioned her with my eyebrows, hardly daring to commit myself to a conversation by using actual spoken words until I'd determined the lay of the land here.

"They was a preacher come by our place in West Virginia a while back. We had Bessie Lou stayin' a spell, till they figured out what t'do with her? Poor chile, she wa'n't right in the head, if you know what I mean. That preacher, he started gittin' mighty suspicious when he took notice of how she di'n't finish her whole glass of milk, she took it and a piece of bread along with her when she done left the breakfast table. He jes' got hisself all riled up when she done it three days in a row, and he made us foller her, and we found out she was leavin' that milk and bread for a big ole black snake under the house. Ooh, wee, the devil was in that snake, he said, and it had her hypnotized. So he made us keep her from bringin' the bread an' milk out to under the house, and wouldn't you know but that poor little girl jes' up and died three days later."

I closed my journal and made an expression I hoped was worthy of her confidence, while calculating the distance from the tree to my van should a speedy exit be required. I had taken this trip to disentangle myself from the brambles of middle-aged folly, not to be accosted with strange tales of boondocks voodoo.

2

"It's them preachers is the work of the devil, if'n you ask me," she concluded. "But I kin tell, you ain't that kind. This here's a nice lady," she informed her husband as he crossed the lawn toward us, wiping his hands on a rag.

"Next week Thursday's our forty-seventh anniversary," the old man said, proudly putting his arm around his wife's waist. "Yup, forty-seven years ago I come drivin' through town . . . "

"He was a trucker, and the handsomest one I ever seen," she grinned, showing several missing teeth. "I tole myse'f that there's the man fer me . . . "

"An' come Thursday, I'm taking her across my lap and smackin' her forty-seven times on the bee-hind for every year of good lovin' she give me," he chuckled.

"Oh, now," she tittered, smacking him gently with the back of her hand, while I shuddered at his proposed means of demonstrating his appreciation for her.

They were on their way to visit their son in Colorado, if their car made it, and meanwhile, until it cooled down, there was no telling how many more of their hillbilly practices I was going to become a captive audience to, if it hadn't been for the appearance of an enormous creature from among the boxes and bundles cramming the back of the station wagon. It plumped itself onto the rolled-down window ledge, its belly slumping over the door on either side, and frowned at us.

"Is that your cat?" I nodded toward their car, having finally found a reason to summon a few spoken words. If I got up to pet what I supposed was indeed a cat, although it probably weighed in at a hefty forty pounds, I'd be that much closer to my getaway car.

"Oh, you don't want to be gittin' too close to Billy," the missus warned me. "Why, when that preacher come through ag'in, Billy took to dislikin' him somethin' powerful. He bent down to pet Billy, and Billy near took his arm off. It was all shredded like. Ha!" she burst out. "Billy can read people, that's what he kin do. I don't reckon that preacher'll be back any time soon!"

Her words followed me to the station wagon, for there was a look in Billy's eyes that drew me toward him. He was one tired old puss. I cupped my hand over his huge head, and he pushed it up into my caress.

"Why, look at Billy takin' to her like that!"

"Have a safe trip," I said, giving Billy a final scratch under the chin and turning toward my van. "Good luck with your car."

"I'm going to say my prayers for you," the old woman said to me. There was something in her voice that made me turn around. She must have been blind in one eye, because it was hazed over, but from her other eye sparkled a beautiful light. "Will you say your prayers for me, too?"

"Yes," I said, suddenly feeling as if an angel had just asked me to watch over her. "Yes, I will."

"We'll say our prayers for each other." And again the light in her eye bathed me in grace.

That hadn't happened to me in a long time, being bathed in grace, being opened to light filling every cell, light creating buoyancy, timelessness, surrender to the embrace of exquisitely comforting rightness and bliss.

She smiled and nodded.

Driving onward, reviewing the encounter, I couldn't help but think that when I got old, I'd hike my sweat pants up over my belly and wear neon green running shoes and never let people know until the last minute that I was blessing their journey from a heart that had never succumbed to ignorance.

2

Please Pass the Healing

Could it be that easy?

"I'm afraid I might have healed someone of cancer," Brooke announced to the six of us sitting around the fireplace in her living room. Running her fingers through her Charlie's-Angel brunette curls, she described how she'd laid her hands on the sufferer and prayed to the universe, to God, to make this person whole. "Then I found out the disease had, like, *disappeared*. But how could *I* have such power?" she beseeched us with a little frowning smile. How could she *not* have such power, I wondered.

She'd not only survived finding her husband hanging from a rafter in the basement of this house, she'd begun to encourage all of us to springboard ourselves from Neale Donald

5

Walsch's God, whose conversations we were gathered to discuss, into creating our own working relationship with the universe. "Oh, don't get me wrong, I would love to discover that this is the new path I'm meant to take!" Her eyes lit up for a moment, and then dimmed. "But even if the miracle *was* really truly the result of my actions and prayers, I mean . . . " she raised her palms in front of her, "it wasn't *me* who did the healing . . . " waving away the ownership of this terrible ability to defy reality, "it was God."

Leaning invisibly from my living-room-present self toward a self that was one dimension over to the right of me, I listened with a little smiling *aha*. Before Brooke could graciously continue to belittle herself, I interrupted her with the insight that had just been whispered to me. "Brooke, if all of us were sitting at the dining room table, and I said to you, 'please pass the butter,' and you asked the person next to you to pass the butter, and then you accepted it and handed it to me, would you have any qualms about the miraculous power of your words or actions?"

She raised her eyebrows, ready to hear more, already hearing more.

"All you did was say to God or the universe, 'please pass the healing,' and then you handed the healing to the person who had asked for it."

The funny little sound she made was a mixture of relief and delight.

I was quite impressed myself with what I'd just said, and besides, I hadn't had this many attentive pairs of eyes on me since I'd brought out the birthday cake for a bunch of five-year-olds a few lifetimes ago. "This applies to you, too, Marilyn," I continued to translate the images being blown at me, iridescent bubbles popping gently into my right brain. "You'd like to be able to trust that what you desire will come to you, right? Even when things don't seem to be unfolding toward what you've chosen for yourself, you'd really like to be able to just relax and have faith, because over and over again, ever since you knew it was possible to express a thought and have it materialize, everything really has turned out according to your best intentions and fondest desires.

"But from what you've told me . . . " At the sight of her expectantly eager attention, I suddenly wanted to wriggle myself out from under the burden of too much wisdom. "You and I do the same thing. I don't just say, 'Please pass the butter,' and then have another bite of delicious food while the butter is on its way from the other end of the table. I *watch* that butter. 'If you could just pass the butter down this side of the table,' I point, 'or, oh, well, okay, if you're going to . . . hey, what are you doing keeping the bu . . . oh, oops, well, you know what? I don't really need the butter after all, I just thought maybe if no one else wanted . . . I mean . . . is anybody ever going to pass me the butter or . . . *what's everybody looking at?*'"

To my delight, everybody laughed. We all got the point at the same time, myself included.

It's as if I was raised in an orphanage or a zoo. But so were my parents, and their parents, who were raised in an environment of stark, artificial scarcity and limitation. We had no *intimacy* with our true parents, our creators, our source, the One who would have loved us so naturally that we would have grown up, like well-nursed puppies with all of their needs met, into creatures full of expectant joy. What we got was alien to our original nature: remote figureheads of authority telling us what the rules were, seeing to it we stayed within manufactured boundaries and got enough manufactured food. We're so impoverished and cowed that we can't believe that asking for something means we'll get it as a matter of course. We think it's a miracle if we ask for something and we get it. We're so impoverished we don't even know we *can* ask. (What do you mean you don't go to the dentist? You just ask your tooth to heal itself? And it does?)

Some of us, like orphans at the window, still have our hunger pressed up to this new world of natural miracles without a clue that if we knock, it shall be opened. Even those of us who are actually sitting at the table in this new dimension watch in drooling awe the family we long to belong to, curing diseases, making money, finding soul mates, talking to angels, passing the butter, potatoes, strawberry-kiwi cream pie, and only slowly, ever so slowly, as we pay attention, does it dawn on us . . .

My nineteen-year-old daughter's old car sputtered and died. She thanked it for a good year of use, waved good-bye as it was towed away, and then paged through *Consumer's Guide* to give herself an idea of what to look for in a newer used car. She narrowed her choices down until she knew exactly what she wanted.

"Okay," I said, "so we're looking for a Toyota Tercel, and it has to have fewer than 70,000 miles on it, and be a '92 or newer, and cost under $4,000."

"And I'd like it to be either silver or teal . . . no, teal," she decided.

"Fawni, this is a used car we're talking about here. We don't get to choose the color!"

"Mm . . . I'd like it to be teal," she smiled, shrugging.

Two days later, I came across an ad in the paper for a '93 Toyota Tercel with 68,000 miles on it for $3800. It was teal.

And it dawned on me.

It can be that easy.

3

One Leg Is Both the Same

Did you ever hear that one? It's the answer to: What's the difference between a duck?

I never knew there were such major differences among ducks, until I got my daughter two for Easter, two motherless incubator ducklings, a yellow one that will eventually turn white and is called what sounded to my uneducated ears like pecan or peekin, and a brown one that will probably look like a mallard but be called a rowan, or so I was informed by the man at Agway, who scooped the ones I pointed at, the two sitting together on top of the feeder tray, into a carton and then handed me a ten-pound bag of Game Starter.

We call them Hewlett and Packard, as they were named by Eli, my once-stepdaughter Raine's seven-year-old son. Or, more often, we call them Ducky, in the high-pitched crooning of maternal invitation, and when we do, they scamper across the floor of the bedroom to the edge of the mesa that is a lap, with their pathetically unformed little wings helplessly and eagerly outstretched, and then they duck (for real), and then they leap, heroically, onto the lap, scrambling and cooing and chirping up the front of the shirt, nuzzling into the neck, preening the hair and earlobes with loving sounds, more endearingly happy to see us than any pet I've ever known. These two ducklings, anyway, make eye contact. They tilt their heads, gaze up at us, talk to us, and settle in for however long we want to be told we're loved.

The two of them are equally affectionate when it comes to making little nesting noises in an armpit, and their differences don't show up when they're following one of us down the hall, their little rubbery footsy flappings doing double time. They both flop down the two steps into the living room, becoming stranded on their backs like frantic beetles if they tumble the wrong way. The pair of them waddle in unison, with necks stretched tall and wings tucked close, past the curious cats, out the door, and across the lawn, cheeping and bumping into each other in their eagerness to keep up with those gargantuan mother strides, on their way to the ten-foot-diameter hose-fed pond. It is here, at the stone and concrete wall that rises about ten inches from the level of the grass, inside of which the water is about twenty inches deep, that we arrive at the difference between a duck called Hewlett and a duck called Packard.

Hewlett, the yellow one, has no interest whatsoever in being picked up and helped over the stone wall of the pond, which is over twice his height. He (I'm guessing when I say "he" or "she" here; until down gives way to feathers, which will show a masculine curve to the tail—or not—they're both the same) does indeed want to get into that pond. Oh yes, Hewlett's been here before and this is what ducks do best, this is duck heaven; nibbling all those strands of slimy algae and those floating dead gnats—how they put to shame that Game

Starter gruel—and ducking under the water, a glory awaited all night in the bathroom, despite the comfort of an old towel. Hewlett can hardly wait to get into that pond. But Hewlett scorns with vocal indignation any attempt to deprive him of the opportunity to test his one-week-old prowess. If he can leap onto a lap by himself, he can leap over this wall. At the sight of a helping hand, he runs as if catapulted at Charlie Chaplin speed. Waddling in fast-forward out of reach, just barely keeping himself balanced with those nubbins of wings, he peeps what sounds like a two year old's outrage when you didn't let him flush the toilet by himself.

Okay, be that way.

How about you, Packard?

Packard, the brown one, looks up at me and lifts her little yellow beak daintily to signal her expectation. She steps calmly into my proffered palm, and, keeping a trusting balance as she glides over the wall on my hand, she surveys the surrounding scenery, eyes the upcoming water with savored expectancy, and remains on my palm until it has been lowered just the right distance into the water so that she can allow the temperature of the water and the temperature of her feet to blend into an uncommonly satisfying experience. Ah. Then she dips her beak into the water, lifts it to the heavens, lets the cool liquid run down her throat, and perhaps in a minute or so, she lowers herself into the pond and happily paddles off after whatever delicacies the surface has to offer today.

And then, noting his absence, she calls to Hewlett.

Who is on the other side of the wall, having taken aim, ducked, and heroically launched himself halfway up the concrete and stone as many times as he has scuttled away from that helping hand in fowl exasperation. When Packard's calls become more insistent, he finally allows that hand to come up under him, but then he's scurrying up that arm and about ready to fall so another hand reaches to steady him and that is so beyond what he is all about that he does fall, on the wrong side of the wall, the grass side, and so the hand is coming at him again, and he jumps it and almost escapes but it's got him and he squirms out of it and *ker-splashes* sideways and full force into the cold water and huffs off peeping loudly that he *told* you but you never listen, and the owner of the hand, me, I suddenly know how God feels.

God/I just wanted to help you over the rough part, and you, little one, made it so easy on both of us by trusting me and yourself, and *you*, little one, made it so hard on both of us by refusing my help.

And I love you both the same.

Only I don't really feel like God, not even when I get Hewlett . . . I get him a rock and put it against the wall so he can negotiate it entirely on his own and aim himself into the water like any duckling with a duck mother would have to do. He paddles off peeping triumphantly that I finally listened. When a duckling does what ducks do best, dives under the water and comes up and raises himself high, flapping tiny unformed wings, and then paddles by in a semicircle cocking his head, looking me right in the eye, and, I swear, smiling, I know I finally did listen, and, duh—passed the butter.

4

Only Bipolar

Bipolarity, I am told by a self somewhere to the left of my present self, is not experienced along a continuum.

(Because I am not bipolar, it can be assumed that I don't know what I'm talking about. But maybe this other self does.)

Imagine not being allowed to live at your own center, your own home. Every time you come from your own center, appear from your home, you are smacked, yelled at, scowled at, or otherwise more seriously discouraged to repeat this uncalled-for antisocial behavior. You are instructed, under penalty of ostracism or starvation, to live in and act from someplace other than your own center, your own home, but the alternative provided for you is a yard full of rubbish, vermin, plastic games, Styrofoam containers, politics, factories . . . you get the picture.

If you are not allowed to live in your own home, which is comfortably messy and cozy and swaying with your own preferences in music and/or silence, and you can't breathe when you try to live in the yard, you have two choices.

(I have known a few bipolar people, and I've just met someone else who might be, and I'm asking one of my selves for this information to see if there's anything worth passing along here.)

Two choices. You can hide deep inside the confines of your home, away from the windows so you won't be seen, pretending not to be home, sneaking out only after dark, and feel totally helpless, powerless, paranoid, and not in control of anything.

Or you can go out there, way out there, beyond the parameters of the yard, to a height from which you can peruse the entire set-up with a critical eye that borders on genius, with a rage and a compassion and a sense of the absurd that fills you up with laughter and scorn, and feel extremely powerful, clued-in, and totally in control.

Being bipolar is not about swinging from one extremity to another along a spectrum of self. It's about shrinking and expanding within and around what is experienced as an insufferable, suffocating no-man's-land where only the numb survive.

Hiding inside one's own place trying not to be seen will obviously lead to feeling unseen, not to mention unwanted, depressed, wondering if one is okay, asking in subtle or manipulative ways, do you find me attractive? Can you spare me a dime? What did I do wrong? Is it okay if I die now? Leave me alone. The world out there sucks. Nothing ever changes. No one loves me. I hate myself. Go away. Don't make me go out there.

But then, there's only so much you can take of that scene. Because, after all, you are alive, and, guess what, you are sane, or you wouldn't be reacting so clearly and obviously the way you'd be expected to react, if you are sane, to an insane dilemma. So you sneak out the back door, crawl through the clones, drones, and automobiles, and reach the high ground and look down and shout, "Come up here with me! Look at that mess! Don't stay there! It's so much better up here, it's amazingly wonderful! Look, space to dance in! You're all crazy! I love you! God loves you! Let's all *fly! We can do anything!* And who was that depressed person in that house down there?"

Well, so, after a while you realize that when you feel *that* good, it's practically impossible to sleep, and besides, whoever might have been dancing with you for a while has left, or been left in, the dust of your whirlwind, and it's getting lonely and the cold stars are too close and down there is your home, and you live there, after all . . . so you drag yourself back through the sneers and pleas, past the proffered numbing medications, and when nobody's looking, you slip into your home, sigh, thinking, it's not so bad being green, or small, or unnoticeable . . . and who was that overblown, fraudulently happy extremist up there on the high ground?

And so the cycle goes.

But, given that you are alive and sane, and your world is divided into three zones, in this illustration, anyway, and it would be intolerable or maybe even impossible to maintain both your life and your sanity repeating these cycles, something has to change, right?

Do you work on changing the feeling that you have no control? That seems reasonable, given you are now an adult and don't have to cower to threats.

Do you work on changing the feeling that you have all the control? That seems reasonable, given that everyone has some kind of say in all of this.

Do you work on changing the middle zone? The way the world is. Help make the intolerable more tolerable. Very reasonable.

So, you *should* be able to stand at the window of your own home in full view, walk out your front door with your chest out, smile at the mailman, and be who you are.

You *should* be able to step out of the limelight, down off the soapbox, out of the studio, away from the dance floor . . . be who you are?

You *should* be able to join in, move politely among the numb, assist in gradual changes . . . ? Become homogenized? Be who you are?

Not.

Buzz. (Thank you for playing.)

The correct answer doesn't begin with "You *should*." The correct answer—correct me if I'm wrong here—is bound to appear when we ask the correct question, which is: What is it really that's driving you nuts?

(I don't know, but I do, over here, and so do you, over there, next to yourself.)

That's it! That's what's driving you nuts.

It's driving you nuts that you are either one or the other of a pair who doesn't get the other one at all. Being bipolar is like being married to a recluse when you're an extrovert; it's like being the Siamese twin of a partier when you're a pooper. But what, you're going to kill one of you off, or substitute part of one of you for part of the other one of you, and you're going to do it in front of the whole group?

And that isn't going to drive you nuts?

What's driving you nuts is that you're only bipolar.

There's much too much of you to survive in such a limited format. Be tri-polar, at least. Be mega-polar, be kilo-polar. Be your whole clan of selves, some of whom disagree, some of whom don't even want to talk with one another, some of whom have great advice, some of whom are greedy, or altruistic . . . .

There are more than three zones to live in! More than you can count! So why choose only two?

Because I have no control! I don't even exist!

Okay. And . . . ?

I control it all. I breathe and the entire universe changes. I live everywhere.

16

Okay. And . . . ?

I don't want to fit into the pigeonholes, I'm unique, I'm a combination of moods and talents and thoughts and strengths and failings like no other on the planet.

Okay! Please pass the string beans and cucumber salad and bacon bits and French vanilla coffee . . . .

Sometimes we just can't force our way toward integration, or any goal, by aiming for it directly. Sometimes we have a better chance of achieving integrity, or whatever it is we desire, if we do exactly what we wouldn't think we ought to do. Like Alice walking backward in the looking glass, if we can see the world as a reflection of ourselves, we can approach it differently. Instead of regarding the problem that needs solving from the outside, get inside it, let it show itself to you, let it guide you into the direction it's already going, even if that seems to be in the opposite direction of the desired end.

Split? Split more. Allow yourself to be fragmented, get to know how fragmented you are, be okay with being fragmented, *enjoy* having lots of selves, and *voila*, or eventually, all the parts add up to a greater whole. Whether segregation is worldwide or individual, allowing all the voices to speak their truths, to be respected for their contributions, to be empowered instead of denied, is to create fertile ground for a garden that benefits from everyone's talents and produces benefits for everyone's well-being.

As each of us listens to the crowd of selves within us and appreciates, befriends, releases from bondage, and allows to be free and expansive each of our inner beings—whether frightened child or angry adolescent or controlling adult or frustrated artist or helpful angel or enlightened soul—we will begin to acknowledge and engage those selves in others, and free them from their numbing armor. We will sit at a table filled with the fruits of our differences and pass them around in abundance.

5

Having Seconds?

There's nothing more disgusting to me than *me* when I'm rummaging through the trash, the waste paper basket, maybe the car ashtray looking for the longest butt. Aha, here's one! A whole quarter inch left on it! Anybody watching? Uncrumple it, smarten it up a bit, dust it off, light it up too close to my nose for comfort, one last drag, hee hee, aah . . .

Hack, hack . . .

Yuck.

I mean, come on, I've decided to quit. It's expensive, unhealthy, gross, and pathetically oral. It's sick.

But why, why, tell me why should I quit, why am I reducing myself to this groveling for the worst of the experience, when I could just go out and buy myself another pack and start fresh with a long clean smooth tasty . . . oh . . . it's such a pleas-ure to kick back after part of my current painting is done and peruse it in comfort, inhaling inspiration, relaxation, flavor, watching with dreamy noninterest the curling blue line join the off-yellow cloud, combining an artistic sense of nonchalance with an adult sense of self-sovereignty . . . .

Fool! Three days you've gone, three whole days you've been a nonsmoker, feeling cleared, energetic, and ready to meet your nonsmoking soul mate at last! What are you doing? You smoked when you were keeping company with pained, deluded souls; none of the people you respect are smokers (not true) (hush!); you're on the threshold of a better world, a disease-free, open-air world of heaven on Earth, and you smell like an ashtray!

I know. I'm bad. I'm sorry. It isn't even the nicotine. I didn't even notice the physical need. It wasn't even hard to quit, as long as I was fasting and doing things I don't normally do. It's those moments when I stop a familiar routine, when cupping a flame to the end of my cigarette settles me in, gives me a moment of time outside of time; it's the contemplation, the something-and-nothingness of peering at the world over the visible release of everything you just took in, then letting it go, drawing from your very blood to exhale it all, noticing it's gone . . . .

Okay, so you love it. So don't quit.

But I don't want to be a smoker!

So there's this other side of being multi-polar. Which is the same as being human, as I see it, or being God, for that matter. Too many sides to every issue. Too many self-images to pick from. How do I choose what I want and stick to it? "Please pass the butter" is just way too simplistic—I mean, okay, I have a steaming baked potato in front of me, obviously I say "Please pass the butter," or maybe the sour cream, but that's about it. Broccoli, cheese, chives. Still, easy to number, and all tasty.

Anybody in here with any answers?

On the issue of smoking?

On the issue of choices.

Ah. Well, the choices should be easy to number and all tasty.

Okay . . . ?

You know, look at a few futures, hone in on one you like, dress it up, tone it down, feel it out. Who or what are you in that future? What about this one? Or is there something better? (They took away years of our lives when they outlawed daydreaming. No matter. We have years now that are ours and no one else's, and, besides, we'd like them to know that they can daydream, too.) Please don't pass your daydream. Stop and look at it. Look at it, fine-tune it until it makes you smile, makes you dare to sparkle. Do you dare? How would it feel to be grinning with someone who is as happy to be here as you are? Laughing with incredulous revelation? Ooh, you say? That one pulled you toward itself? Well, then, baby. Please pass the passionate-peach-flavored nectar of life.

Wait a minute; did I just dare to dream something? I don't know. I think I see it, but it could be one thing or it could be another.

Having second thoughts? Let yourself listen. What you want is trying to talk to you.

I think I'm scared.

You don't feel safe? Why not? Would your choice lead to pain?

No. It would not be acceptable to experience pain. No more pain. I don't want to die that many more times. Once. Once more will do, with grace, with ease. I want to die only once more in this lifetime, and I want to die happy. I want to die looking back and saying *yes!*

So do what you want to do because you want to do it. Maybe life isn't a path. Maybe it's a dance. Maybe the dance floor has all these panels that light up when you step on them, and whenever you step on one that says *yes,* you just slowly, surely, fluidly dance that way, until you drop dead happy. Anything you do, if you do it from where you live, from home, from the center, from your hunger, from your desire for fulfillment, not only changes the yard by the very glow of your presence when you step outside, it changes you into a person of 360-degree perception. You can see the whole yard, the whole dance floor. All areas are illuminated by your grace. When you are no longer hiding from yourself, nothing is hidden from you. When you no longer fear yourself, nothing generates fear in you. How do you know what you want? How do you stick to it? There's no need to stick to it. If something on the table smells good, ask to have it passed your way, and when it's on your plate, try it. This *isn't* the orphanage or the zoo. You don't have to eat everything on your plate, even if you put it there. But if you feel like having seconds, well, then, by all means, please do, have seconds.

6

Kosovo

There they sit at their table, grabbing everything, hoarding, shouting, screaming, stomping, beating and pushing away from the table their own brothers and sisters.

In this country, generally speaking, though many of us may be so impoverished we hardly dare ask for anything, most of us can hardly fathom the spiritual and emotional starvation level that reduces human beings to snarling beasts frothing with murderous hatred and greed.

It happened in World War II, but it wasn't portrayed in vivid detail on TV, so all we knew here in the States was that war is hell, man's inhumanity to man is the greatest treachery there is, and except for the families whose menfolk came home maimed, or didn't come home at all, that was pretty vague.

Holocaust stories and films are horrific, but for most Americans, as appalling as they are, they're diluted, second-hand.

Vietnam was televised, and war is hell became a little more present and specific, but we had so many mixed messages and mixed emotions about that war, we hardly knew how to acknowledge or make sense of who or what was the enemy, what was being fought over, or who could benefit if what was done.

Kosovo is right here, right now, in our living rooms, and pretty freaking self-evident. People are being shoved over the edge. Raped. Slaughtered.

When the subject came up in our "book study" group last night (euphemism for "life study" by now), a pall of grief and guilt descended on all of us. We're okay, and they're not. What can we do? What do you do when you're wondering if you should change jobs for greater soul-satisfaction, and your neighbors are killing each other? On a global level, or a neighborhood one, what do you do when you see other human beings suffering?

I can't answer this. Not for anyone else, anyway. I'm just trying to answer it for myself. A scene comes to mind from the second Billy Jack movie. A father had chopped off his child's hand in a moment of uncontrolled rage. The people who cared were counseling the child, of course. But they were also counseling the father. They were addressing the ungodly rage, self-loathing, and guilt of the father. They were surmising that despite such a demonic act, there was also, in this crazed, despondent human being, someone who was in excruciating need of being recognized and cared about. The premise was that punishment would only amputate the possibility of forgiveness along with the hand. Without both of them healing, neither could ever really heal. So father and son were being given the opportunity to re-create a near-death-blow into a life transformation.

When I was married to a man who was so angry and so unhappy with himself that he threatened to go off into the woods and never come back, and actually walked out the door with the intention of killing himself almost every other week, it took me two years to learn that nothing I could offer—not my pleas, my attempts to love away the pain, my rage, my sane explanations, my exasperation, my concerned attentive listening—none of it made any difference. His suicidal drive continued to plague him from the dark depths of his unacknowledged nation of selves.

It was a hard lesson for me, someone who had spent much of her life caring for other people, to have to kick him out of my life to save myself. It was also a cure. He cured me of not valuing my own embarrassing, frightened, banshee-woman selves, my own untapped well of ways to live my life. And because I was grateful to him for that, I continued to be open to talking with him after we were divorced. The last time we talked, three months ago, we sat on my lawn, and he asked my permission to go off into my woods and never come back. He'd reached the end, he was making that choice, and he was at peace with it. I did something I had never been able to do while we were together. I calmly told him he had my blessing. I knew he loved these woods, and if he wanted to leave his body on this land and go to the Other Side, I understood and wished him good passing.

He has not called or visited since, but yesterday there was a package under my mailbox, a gift. No words, no signature, just a meaningful gift addressed to me in his handwriting.

So, where Kosovo is concerned, where a next-door family feud is concerned, I suspect that the answer is the opposite of what I'd expect it to be.

Not that that kind of suggestion hasn't been around for quite some time. Love thine enemy. Turn the other cheek.

If your neighbor is yelling at her kids, and you don't know how to make a difference in her life, make one in yours. Send her your prayers, which might make more of a difference than you'll ever know, and then move to a better location, because you have the right to—and the world *needs* you to—choose your own happiness, untainted with guilt.

If those Nazi-hearted Serbs are raping young women, mass-murdering innocent families, then what are we waiting for? *Kill* the damned bastards.

That's my answer. For myself. Vent my outrage. Offer into the planet's atmosphere my acceptance of a disease destroying itself so the rest of humanity can be healthy. That's part of my answer.

I'd had a pea-sized cyst on my shoulder, about a quarter of an inch under the flesh, for about two years when it finally occurred to me that I could instruct my body to get rid of it. Body, I said, make this cyst surface and erupt. Nothing happened for a couple of weeks. And then what had felt like a frozen pea under the frequently curious pressure of my finger began to feel like a cooked lima bean. Oh, I said, sorry, body, you can't do what I demanded. You're going to dissolve this thing under the surface and carry the toxic remains out through the normal channels. I should have just *asked* in the first place, and trusted that you'd figure out a solution. Thank you. Within a week after the softening, the cyst was gone.

Kosovo, lest we lose our perspective, is a few thousand diseased cells in a body of over six billion cells. As part of the consciousness of the body, any of the rest of us can, if we choose, align ourselves with the desire to have the disease eliminated, and then let it go, let those cells that do that kind of thing take care of it. They can come from anywhere in the body, they know when they're called, and they know their job, whether it's to pray for or to prey upon the predators, whether it's to provide a safe haven for the innocent or to alert the world.

Me, I'm not a white corpuscle. Okay, so maybe I look like one on my better days, but I prefer to see myself as a nerve cell that coordinates eye to hand to create art.

Let each of us do what we are best equipped to do, and we can't help but maintain the health of this miraculously designed body that we call humanity.

7

Life's Little Mysteries

Speaking of cysts, I once felt a hard little BB-sized nodule on the tip of my elbow. What is this? I asked, rolling it around under the loose skin. It was so close to the surface that when I pressed my thumbnail to it, it popped out. It *was* a BB. A bright, shiny copper BB. How in all the world did a BB end up in my elbow?

I thought back to the one time I'd been hit by a BB. A friend, or so I called him at the time (but would a friend do what he did?), shot me in the rear end with a BB gun from six feet away. It stung. But I never checked to see what happened to the BB. Did it bounce off? Did it make a tiny hole in my jeans? Did it penetrate my flesh? How else could a BB have arrived in my elbow unless it had somehow entered my body somewhere? But could it have traveled from my rear end all the way through, what, blood vessels and muscles up to my shoulder and down my arm? Wouldn't that be just too amazing for words? What a journey, one that would have taken the twelve years between my having been hit and the emergence of the BB. How could I have been carrying something around inside me for so long, something I didn't even know was there until it came out?

This is one of the mysteries to which I will probably never find the answer.

8

Any Way

Two years before my daughter was born, I had two abortions with her father within a few months. I was using birth control, but something more powerful than spermicide was at work, and yet, we just weren't ready. He needed to spend a year with another woman. I was already a single mom, and I needed, big time, to spend a year with some of the selves I had locked away in my dungeon. We got back together, not even really sure why, until one day, he put his arms around me and said, "Let's make a baby." My eyes grew wide. "For real?" I was *so* ready for this to happen. "Yeah." Neither time before had I experienced a knowing of conception, but this time, even before the normal signs showed up, we both knew who was on the way. As we sat in front of his woodstove one evening, we each saw, at the same time, with our third eye, a young woman in her twenties who looked a little like his sister and a little like my sister.

When she was two, our daughter asked me, "'Member, Ma, when I was up in the sky and I decided to be a little girl and come in your body?" I didn't even remember her ever having used the word *decided* before. *She* had decided. When she was three, she asked me about her cousin, "How come I'm the same age as her, Ma? I wanted to be older than her."

"How much older, Fawni?" I asked.

"Two years," was her response. She had obviously planned on arriving two years before we were ready. When she was in tenth grade, however, she remarked that she was glad she was the age she was, because she knew no one in the higher grades that she could relate to as well as she could to her closest friends, who were all in her grade. Now that she is nearing twenty, her father and I, who both feel blessed by her presence in our lives, see the same young woman we saw that night by the woodstove.

There was another abortion between us when I sensed we would not be staying together. I asked whoever wanted to come in to please find another way to be part of my life. I couldn't tell if this someone was male or female, or even one of each, because we'd each had dreams about a boy and a girl. I had heard the name Eli, but I didn't tell anyone, because we weren't going to be opening the door this time. So it was none of my doing when my stepdaughter Raine, nine years later, named her son Elijah. We all call him Eli.

My daughter's father is now with a wonderful woman who has a daughter the same age as Eli. Emma, who loves Peter like a father—she hardly knows her own—is so much like Eli, he says, the same kind of energetic, extremely bright, funny, dramatic child, that he's sure they would hit it off immediately if they ever met.

I wonder if there were two souls who wanted to come through that last time. I wonder if both of them managed to do so according to their own needs.

"So, anyway, my dear," I say to the very young woman sitting beside me on the couch, as she wipes her tears from her cheeks, "if you have to eliminate a bit of flesh from your body at this time, if you have to drink some teas to flush out a bad timing or even go the barbaric route of having stainless steel instruments do the job, it won't be fun, but it certainly doesn't have to cause you guilt or grief. Just communicate with whoever wants to be in your life with you, just explain your predicament, and invite him or her to join you at another time."

The light comes on in her eyes, she summons her own wisdom and strength, and she knows she's going to survive this ordeal, because she has a new perspective on the size of it within the size of her lifetime.

Fortunately, I've been able to say something else as well. A young friend of mine, who had already had an abortion with the same man with whom she was now pregnant again, sat on my couch, distraught.

"Why the tears?" I asked.

"Because I have to get another abortion. He's not ready for this."

I sized her up—her exceptionally maternal nature, her lack of plans for the future, her willingness to take care of herself if she had to—and I offered with a shrug, "You could have the baby."

She looked at me, her eyes widening, and she said, softly, "I could have the baby." She said it again, with dawning acceptance. "I could have the baby!" And then she said it a third time, with elation, and I saw her future roll out in front of her, the joy of motherhood blossoming into a precious friendship with her child.

As it turns out, he was ready enough; he's never had anything so wonderful happen to him in his life as the birth of his daughter. Even if they don't stay together, they won't ever not have this bright-eyed, sweet-smiling girl between them. She looks like she knows they both needed her as much as she needs each of them. I tend to think she's right.

"Do you know why I smiled when you runned over that bird, Ma?" my son asked me when he was three, seeing how I was cringing behind the steering wheel.

"No, why, Boogie?" (God is my co-pilot. I call him Boogie.)

"Because even though you did that, I love you anyway."

Abortion is such an emotionally and politically charged issue—as well it should be, because it is a traumatic way of manipulating reality. The day will come when women will know how to realign their futures with their loving intentions. They will know that the instruments they need to redesign a regretted choice are not made of steel, but of conscious thoughts. They will know that appealing to the universe in the best interest of everyone involved includes their own best interest as they determine it for themselves, for they too *are* the universe, unfolding itself toward perfection. In the meantime, as we learn to rise above our fears and into our natural power, what our society's daughters deserve to know is that they *can* redirect, into another time or through another door, the entry of another soul, by agreement. If someone wants to be with you that much, they might not want to take no for an answer, but they will certainly hear "not now"—and they will love you anyway.

9

Before, During, and After

"Can I eat dis g'een booberry, Ma?" my daughter asked me when she was two and a half. She was sitting on the kitchen table, in that way kids have, with her feet jutting out at right angles from beside a diapered heiny. She had finished chopping her play dough snake into cookies and sending them off on their designated assignments—rolling them off the table with exclamations of "One fer Dad, here it comes, whee! One fer Ma. Wheee!" and she had just discovered, in one of the bowls of fruit I kept filled on the kitchen table, her first unripe blueberry.

"I don't think it would taste very good," I cautioned her, remembering when she'd stuck a live black beetle into her mouth not long before. I'd heard the crunch and turned around just in time to see her mouth gaping open like a cavern, out of which was sliming to the floor crushed beetle goo with legs. "It isn't ripe," I explained its color, pointlessly, I was sure, because why should that stop her from her scientific explorations?

She rolled the tiny orb around between her dexterous little thumb and forefinger, considering its possibilities. "Can I stick it up your nose?"

This was the same child who had been singing to herself in the bathtub when she didn't know I was listening? I'd been out in the hall, putting away the towels, and I paused, in awe, hardly believing my ears.

"We are all so conscious. We know everything. But we just like to play along. We are all so conscious. But we like to play."

I shouldn't have been surprised. By then she'd already asked me if I remembered when she decided to come into our lives. She'd already been telling me about her past lives. "I was in a boat wif my baby and de on'y man I loved. I jumped in de water, but den I climbed on de boat, up de stairs on de side, an' I was ho'ding my on'y baby I had, and de on'y man I loved was on de boat too. We had a house in Canyafornia."

When my son Eric, who is seven years older than Fawni, was four, he too made up a chant.

"I love you, Ma, whole wide as the world," he would say, and then he would start singing. "I love you and you love me, just on the way . . . to heavenly light. We love each other, just on the way . . . to heavenly light." Heavenly light. From where he'd remembered that, I couldn't guess.

When he was ten, he told me from where. He was sitting on the floor among his Legos, and what he was saying was so out of context, I grabbed a pen and wrote it down. Gazing into some other dimension, he'd started speaking in a deepened, monotone voice. *We were brought here from another part of the universe. Humanity was planted on this planet. But also, some of us have traveled here spiritually. We actually live long lives as spirits. Each human lifetime is equal to one day in the life of who we are as spirits.*

"You will not stop dreaming, Mom, for another two life-times, but that is only two days. Only two days.

"Life is Time and Time is Life and Life is Death and Death is Life.

"It is hard to be in this body and to do the homework I have to do to fit in, but I have to do it so that I will appear to belong, and so that I can fulfill my purpose.

"Dreaming is nothing more than memories. Memories. Memories. Life is Time and Time is Life and Life is Death and Death is Life.

"Human lifetimes can go on for billions of years, but that is still only a small amount of time in the lifetime of a spirit. One spirit can expand to include many beings. It can even expand to include the whole universe.

"I am starting not to be able to remember who I am.

"Time is Life and Life is Time and Death is Life and Life is Death."

The next day I asked him about what he'd said. He didn't know what I was talking about. He'd known it was about to happen, and it had. He'd forgotten.

My daughter, however, still remembers what she saw when she was almost three. I'd been in my studio, and I returned to the house assuming that Fawni and her dad would both be asleep, but she was waiting for me in the living room.

"Where was you, Ma?" she asked.

"I was in the studio, writing, Fafi. What are you doing here all by yourself in the dark?"

"Der was a man here for to see you. For to give you a hug. But he coulden find you."

"A man?" I hadn't heard a car on the driveway.

"Yeah, a purpo man." She was quite serious.

"You mean, he had a purple light around him?" I tried to clarify for myself what she'd just experienced.

"Yeah, like dat. An' he was here for to give you a hug. He showed me a place where der was lots of little childrens. He gave me a seal. Den he went out de door."

The next evening, as she came prancing out of the bathroom in her nightie, with me right behind her, she stopped and pointed at the other end of the long hallway. "Der he is, Ma. Der's de purpo man."

I stooped down beside her and peered, with much too much effort, down the dimly lit hall. "I wish I could see the way you do," I whispered.

I still don't know who the purpo man was.

My father had died two years before Fawni was born. He'd been at home, bedridden, for a month, growing weaker daily from the lung cancer. He'd gathered his family around, my mother, his sister, my brother and sister, and had spoken to us about many things, about how much we meant to him, about what he'd left unfinished, about what he'd like us to do. And then, smiling gently, he told us all that where he was going, we couldn't follow, not yet, but he was looking forward to it, because he knew that death was simply a transition into the next stage of life.

A few hours before he died, he gazed ahead, his eyes glowing, his face softening, and he exclaimed, "Oh! It is so beautiful!"

"What, Arieto, what?" his sister asked.

"It is so beautiful." He fell asleep, curled up like an infant, his last rasping breath followed by silence. As I knelt beside his bed and stroked his head gently, I expected that he was entering the place he had seen that was so beautiful. I didn't expect ever to see him again.

But he visited all of us afterwards. Comparing notes a few days later, we discovered that he had visited each of us in a dream, on the same night, wearing a maroon smoking jacket, a gift he'd never worn again after having tried it on to please his guest. He wore it while dream-visiting, we were sure, so that we'd comment on it and comprehend.

Among his things, I found three small metal shapes, key-sized, one of which I sent to my sister, one that I gave to my brother, and one that I kept for myself. I placed my little woman-shaped key on a slightly protruding rock in the stone wall of a bedroom in my house, where it perched for sixteen years. Five years ago, I leaned back from a painting I'd just finished, feeling pleased enough to consider selling it, and wished that my father, who had been a successful artist, could have been there to advise me. Had I attained enough mastery to begin a career in art?

Ping! went something behind me. Electrified, I turned around. The little key perched on the wall had fallen—or jumped—or been pushed—onto my desk. I was filled with a silently billowing, encouraging *yes*.

The painting sold, the first of many.

But was it my father that Fawni saw when she was little?

It had been twenty years since I'd refused to marry Parker, but now that everything was falling apart in my life, I needed someone to tell me what to do, and he'd always been straight with me. I dialed his mother's number, hung up, and dialed again, my heart pounding. "Hi, Mrs. D., I'm an old friend of Parker's, and I was just wondering . . . "

"Oh, my dear," she said sadly, "Parker died."

I was stunned. After several attempts at suicide, the man I had loved had fallen to his death from the penthouse of a tall building, eleven days after Fawni was born.

I didn't find this out until two years after Fawni saw the purpo man. And it wasn't until years later that he started writing messages to me, with his own peculiar twist of words, in his own handwriting, through my pen as I made entries into my journal. Occasionally I could hear his voice, sharing information from the Other Side. Finally he asked me to let his son know that he loved him. I sent a brief note to his son (whom I'd never met, since he'd been born after Parker and I had parted), telling him that I'd known his father, and that he could write to me if he wanted to know more, but six months passed with no response. Then, as I was standing on the beach at ten o'clock one September morning, saying goodbye to the ocean at the end of a brief vacation, a tall column of white light appeared next to me, radiating joy. I knew it was Parker, but I didn't know why he was filled with joy, until I reached into my mailbox three days later and pulled out a letter from his son, postmarked 10:00 A.M., three days earlier. He was ready to hear about his father.

All of these experiences had thinned the veil between dimensions, had opened my world to the abundance of love and wisdom and guidance available from people not yet incarnate or no longer incarnate, but it wasn't until a year ago that their generously loving presence was so clearly and specifically manifested for me that I could never doubt or question it again.

My friend Marilyn, sitting at my kitchen table one morning, had told me that every time she thought of her mother, Dorothy, who had died when Marilyn was in her twenties, she would find a penny. Right there on the floor she had just vacuumed, or right there on the porch she had just swept clean, a penny. Was her mother reassuring her? Letting her know she could hear Marilyn's thoughts?

Our conversation went on to other more pressing matters. Marilyn's daughter had recently escaped from the deadening boredom and confinement of compulsory concrete walls to breathe in the manna of a beautiful day. The school authorities were calling it truancy and threatening suspension. Her son had been summoned into court to defend himself against a false accusation. We talked about how much our parents had given us, compared to what they'd been given, and how much we wanted to give our children, even more than our parents had known how to give us. "Marilyn," I assured her, "you *will* be able to make use of your best mediation skills to defend your children, in both situations. And besides," I added, "Dorothy will be with you."

Suddenly there was a spinning sound on the floor. We stared at each other with widening eyes.

"Did you hear that?"

"I heard it!"

"Where is it?"

We shoved our chairs back and looked around on the floor, and there it was, right where we had heard it come to rest. A penny.

A penny from heaven.

Marilyn's daughter was not suspended from school.

When Marilyn and her son walked into the courtroom, she saw the outline of an angel's wing glowing behind the judge. Not only did the judge recognize her son's defense, the false accuser was duly reprimanded.

A month later, as I was washing the dishes, pondering a situation that seemed to require a little angelic assistance, I appealed to Marilyn's mother to help out if she could. I rinsed the last mug out under the faucet, when suddenly a penny ricocheted around the bottom of the sink as if it had been tossed there. I was almost surprised. But by then, really, I wasn't. I just smiled and thanked Dorothy for hearing me.

Although I'm still not certain of the identity of the purpo man, I am certain, after having been taught by my children what to look for and listen to and believe in, and after having been the recipient of pennies from heaven, that those who love us are with us, *always*—before, during, and after what we call life.

And they are always abundantly generous with their loving guidance.

"Fawni, you have to be the sweetest little girl I've ever known," her dad told his three year old as she sat on his lap. She leaned back from him, studied him a moment, as if assessing his ability to handle the truth, and retorted, "No, I don't *have* to be."

I hid my smile, secretly enjoying the wisdom of the Goddess in the words of a child whose soul, like yours, like mine, is eternal.

10

Silver Senses

I awoke with a start. My silver she-wolf was onto something and wanted me to follow her.

The first time she came to me was the morning after my third abortion. I surfaced from a long, restful, deep sleep, but before I could open my eyes, I saw a field mouse scampering through a forest fire. Keeping my eyes closed, I watched the tiny creature zigzag through the flames. She leaped over patches of blackened, smoking ash, scurried along the broad highway of a mossy fallen tree, and clambered down to the edge of a rushing stream. After testing the shore for an easier passage, she finally just plunged in and paddled across, fighting to keep abreast of the current. Drenched dark and slick, she slowly wended her way up through the enormous boulders on the other side. Halfway up the slope of the mountain she stopped and collapsed, exhausted, gasped a few tiny breaths, and expired. Her damp brown pelt split open, and out of it, impossibly, stretched a young, gangly, dazed wolf. Her silver fur sparkled in the sunlight. She steadied herself on her long wobbly legs, shook herself clear, looked around, sniffed the air, and began to climb toward the heights above her. She was beautiful.

A few days after my vision, I opened the front door of my house and nearly stepped on a little brown field mouse crouching by the woodpile. I kneeled down, and because it didn't run off, I picked it up. There seemed to be no blood, or any reason for it to be so docile. It lay in the palm of my hand, looking up at me, took a tiny last breath, and died.

The silver she-wolf came to me again—not as a vision, though—not as a scene that I viewed from a distance as an outsider—but as an animal part of me that rolled herself out of my body and alerted me to follow her. I had the sense, not of having information delivered to me, but of being pulled toward something going on in this reality. Each time she drew me to another place, I'd had the reality of my invisible visit confirmed within a short period of time, so I'd come to trust her sense of urgency.

She sniffed the ground, following a trail, and started digging frantically at a flagstone engraved with the word Montana, until she'd managed to push the stone aside and dive under it. I followed her, emerging within a fraction of a second in front of my sister's yellow cottage in the outskirts of Bozeman. My wolf was already pushing through the front door. Keeping up with her, I followed her into my sister's bedroom, where Celia was lying on her futon, her cheeks wet with tears. The wolf licked her face, whining comfortingly, and then looked back at me.

I opened my eyes onto my own bedroom and looked at the clock. Two hours earlier in Montana . . . it would be 4:30 in the morning there. So what. I dialed her number . . . and left her a message.

Three hours later she returned my call. "I heard the phone ring when you called," she said. "I just didn't want to answer it, because I was crying."

She'd just broken up with the man in her life.

We had a good heart-to-heart talk.

11

The Stories You'll Tell

When I e-mailed my sister a profoundly soulful poem that had been floating around on the Web, entitled "The Invitation," she told me she'd already read it to a gathering of women, all of whom were as moved as we were by the insights of its Canadian author, Oriah Mountain Dreamer. If you'd like to read it, you can type her name into your search engine and find not only her original version, but also how to get a copy of her book by the same title.

The poem reads like an ultra-metaphysical personals ad. Each line tears away at the wrapping of a packaged image and seeks to uncover a deeper requisite for a vital relationship. The poet isn't interested in age, occupation, or zodiac sign. She wants to know if the "you" she's addressing dares to dream, to take risks, to be foolish, to be with pain, to overcome struggle, to shout Yes at the moon, to find replenishment from within.

There's one line that has been singing itself like a mantra into my mind—it's so unlike what I once thought I was looking for in someone I wanted to be able to trust.

It doesn't interest me if the story you are telling is true. I want to know if you can disappoint another to be true to yourself, if you can bear the accusation of betrayal and not betray your own soul.

My mind wanted to dance with the words, twirl them around and look at them from every angle, they rang so true.

Not telling the true story could range anywhere from the American government keeping UFO information from the public to save its own face and maintain its own illusory power, to a Mexican storyteller relating the triumphant victory of an ancestor's fight against injustice even though he actually died not a hero but a victim, for the sake of the listeners' resultant pride in their countrymen. There are lots of reasons for not telling the true story. But—can you alter the truth you once believed in because the soul you save will be your own?

Having read that poem and having listened to the confession of someone who was involved in a twelve-step program, I dreamed I was working in a café. Instead of washing two dirty forks, I just threw them away. My act was not witnessed but was deduced by one of the owners of the establishment, Captain Jean Luc Picard of *Star Trek*. He recommended that a meeting of the staff be held to discuss my mistake, because it was wasteful to throw away the flatware. I was expected to confess my mistake, and everyone would offer their insights, and we would all carry on knowing one another better. Picard was the wise patriarch of my psyche, outlining the "new generation" of workable rules. I, however, decided not to confess.

I went to great lengths to hide the two forks at the bottom of the dumpster, and then to retrieve them and slip them into my pocket so I could pretend at the meeting that I never threw them away, I just accidentally misplaced them. That was going to be my story, and the matriarch of the establishment, an older, brown-skinned woman who has appeared to me in my dreams before, watched me, silently, until she understood my motive: I knew I'd made a mistake, and I knew I wouldn't be wasteful again, but I chose to have the others believe of me that I was careless rather than both irresponsible and a liar.

I chose not to follow the external rules, but to design my own internal ones. I did it not because I intended to alienate or hide myself from the others—I really wanted to continue to be able to work there and be part of the group—but because what I needed most out of the situation was to own my own soul, by making up my own rules and by choosing how I wanted to be seen by others. The matriarch said nothing, just nodded, and the story was accepted.

The person who'd bared his soul in front of a group of fellow confessors had been in the dream as one of the staff members, so I mentioned it to him.

"What you're telling me, it seems," he said, "is that sometimes it's important to put your truth out there, to learn to forgive yourself through the forgiveness of others. But sometimes you're better off owning the responsibility of forgiving yourself, learning from your mistakes by yourself, instead of giving that responsibility away?"

"I think so," I said.

"Hmm, yes, that is very helpful to me right now," he answered, and he didn't tell me why, which was totally cool.

Can you be true to yourself even though by doing so you are forced to disappoint someone? Someone who could answer yes to that question is someone I know I could trust—to have no expectations, no manipulations toward his own desired ends, to be beyond blame and forgiveness, to be fully alive and well in his own reality, to be spontaneously true to his own whims and purpose, and to allow me to be true to mine.

Thanks, Oriah. If we don't know what there is to ask for, how can we ask for it?

Please pass me your story, not the way it was or should

have been, just the way it's true for you right now, even if tomorrow it changes.

Let's hope tomorrow it changes.

How many times mine has changed. Not just because the story I tell you would not be the same story I would tell another. (How could it be? Some of my story fits into some of your spaces, and some of your places are filled with your own story and have no room for mine.) But also because the story I tell myself changes, depending on whether I'm a student of psychology and seeing my history from the viewpoint of a victim of environmental influences; or a student of empowerment, seeing the path I've traveled as directed by my own soul's choices; or of sociology, the expression of a culture; or of past life history, the amender of karma; or of Spirit, the God-Goddess experiencing anything and everything through and with everyone; or no student at all, just me, ad-libbing as I go.

Are you able to be true to your own soul even in the face of an accusation of betrayal? You can, but only if you trust the accuser's soul to fend for itself. If you don't trust the purposefulness of her soul, if you can't bear for her to falsely accuse you of being the source of her pain until she discovers it within herself, if you protect someone from your truth, you deprive her of her own chance at personal power. You fill in from the outside what is really needed from the inside.

Yes, I am betraying you. I am betraying your expectations of me. You stand betrayed. What are you going to do about it? I've been betrayed, thank goodness, because now I know my own strength, and I pass the gift on to you. Do with it what you will.

Of course, you don't have to say that part out loud. Unless you want to.

Do with this betrayal whatever you need to do with it.

What, pass it on? Betray someone else?

If by doing so you are forced to honor yourself, to come home to yourself, to live from your own center, yes, because the trust and compassion and love you develop for yourself and everyone else are so much deeper than that layer of false charity it's so easy to hide behind and to stay numb and trapped behind.

Oh, well that's a relief.

Isn't it? Really, you don't get hardened. How can an act of love harden you?

And then, too, it seems to me that the final outcome of your having chosen, just once, to betray another rather than yourself is that you prefer never to have to betray *anyone* again. You get honest. You trust honesty. You detect variations on honesty. You find honesty to be the most creative way of handling everything. Only through honesty do you never betray your true self again, and only through honesty do you truly have an impact on a reality meant to be Real.

12

Light Worker

Light Worker wanted. No heavy lifting without antigravitational assistance. May have been accused of being an idealist. Will be trained to revise that accusation into a life purpose. Anyone not having suffered disillusionment is not qualified. Pay is not guaranteed. Satisfaction is.

Hmm. Sounds like a humble enough vocation.

That is, until I meet a man whose third eye was opened when he was six years old by gentle beings, who has since channeled spiritual guidance and healing, who sometimes sees angels and auras, and who photographs light pouring in over a windowsill and down onto the floor because he can influence his camera without even trying. A man who, when he speaks of the Light, re-creates the memory of it, the reality of it, like a tsunami rising in my bloodstream, and yet, he is also no stranger to poverty, doubts about his future, messy relationships, or disillusionment.

When such a man stands before me, about to step into his van and looking everywhere but into my eyes, and says that in the last few weeks so many of the things he has been waiting for have materialized, including having met this special lady who has something deep and beautiful inside her, when such a man, himself the materialization of what I didn't even want to admit I'd been waiting for, says to his van, "In maybe ten thousand people there is one Light Worker, and in ten thousand Light Workers, there is one like her," I find myself backing away from a brief awkward hug, waving shyly, and running into my house overcome with so many mixed emotions that it takes me days to sort them out.

Yes! is what I cheer to my daughter when I get inside the house, punching the air in triumph, jumping up and swinging from the ceiling.

Hmm, that makes me one in a hundred thousand, I calculate as I lie in my bed alone that evening. Hey, what happened to one in a million? (Evidently a Light Worker needn't excel in math.)

Finally someone sees the real me! I wake up in a swoon the next morning.

I've just been handed a staggering wheelbarrowful of gold nuggets. Couldn't he maybe just hand them to me one at a time, or is this supposed to last me another whole month? I wonder the next day when I don't hear from him.

Yikes, what an order to have to live up to, I cringe when the weight of it sinks in.

One of the most knock-me-flat, get-it-right lessons I've had to learn in the past few years is that you just can't give someone else a knock-me-flat, get-it-right lesson if he doesn't want it. So I retreated into my art. Let the world do whatever it wants to do. Come holocaust or high water I'm sitting right here and painting my little paintings. Then I was asked if I'd like to join this book study group, and since conversations with God is something I used to find myself having a lot of once, I said okay. And I got inspired to start writing down some of the thoughts I came home with. And I got even more inspired when several of the other people in the group started sharing what they'd been writing. And we all started inspiring each other to take another look at our lives and decide how we wanted to re-create them for ourselves. And lo and behold, some of them started manifesting such amazing things as a trip to Greece to meet Neale Donald Walsch; a house that was even better than the one that got sold to someone else; and a job realignment that answered a need and a prayer.

Meanwhile, my sister, who has also been having conversations with God, e-mailed me that she'd just met this terrific man—through the personals on the Web. Oh, yuck, I thought, is this what humanity has come to? I certainly wouldn't want to meet a man that way. I don't know if I really want to meet a man at all. I mean, yeah, Oriah's poem did have me reconsidering what to ask for if I did want to ask for a man in my life, and mostly I would want someone who was easy to be with . . . but I don't know, I really don't want to lose myself in another relationship.

So I e-mailed my sister back: How exactly did you find the personals on the Web? She gave me instructions. I looked at the personals. Oh yuck, I thought, this is too *gross*. These people are sickos, I said to myself, night after night for two or three weeks as I browsed through Yahoo and Lycos and Excite until two or three in the morning.

Well, when you begin to notice that your entire social life consists of conversations with God every Tuesday night and clicking on photos of pathetically lonely-looking men every Friday and Saturday night, you begin to ask yourself, "What am I doing here? Just what exactly is it that I'm doing here? I have to get myself straightened out here. I have an art career to attend to. I have to figure out how to get my art on the Web. That's what I have to do."

So even when I clicked on this one photo and read the blurb and my heart started racing, I told myself it was because this man said he was creating a Web site. He couldn't really be all those things he said he was. Who would say in a personals ad that he was shy, had never been to college but had studied in the ethereal planes, had never traveled, except out of body, and was looking for someone to share popcorn with? Who would say he was a spiritual healer, for God's sake? What kind of a spiritual healer would put an ad in the personals accompanied by a photo of himself with two heads? But he lived only twenty minutes away, and he knew how to create a Web page.

Our first phone conversation flowed into two hours of easy, eager, awkward, enlightening communication punctuated with silences full of electrifyingly sweet intensity. I finally had to tell him that if we were going to continue this conversation, I was going to have to ask him to hold on a minute—I'd had to pee for the last hour. He said okay. We decided to meet the next day—so that he could help me get my art on the Web. Oh, that's right! *That's* what this is all about, I reassured myself.

And it was, thank you, God, about getting my art on the Web, and about being inspired to move into a new area of art, and about being reminded that I was born an idealist and that it's never too late to be and do what you were born to be and do.

God—the universe, the Goddess, Spirit, the All, the I AM—answers to any nickname, really, and answers even if you don't know exactly how to pose the question, and what's more, when you answer one of God's ads, you're in for a nice surprise.

Accepting the role of Light Worker, accepting it humbly and not taking it lightly but not taking it too seriously, either, means you've said okay to having the Light smiled into you, day after day, so there's plenty to pass around. That's it. That's all there is to it! Oh my God. Easy!

13

One Sex Is Both the Same

Ducks grow at a visible rate, I can now inform you. They are bigger in the evening than they were in the morning. In one week they grow from two ducklings being able to nestle in the palm of one hand to one duckling filling the nest of two hands. In one month they grow from being soft fuzzy nestlers to having smooth crisp feathers and wary independence.

And ducks respond to gender attitude distinctions.

Packard, whom I've always regarded as female, has turned out to be so, a lovely dark-brown-patterned, graceful, feminine creature with shimmering purple-blue-green rectangles bordered in white and black on her wings. She has gentle eyes, doe eyes. When I lie down on the lawn, she is the one who leads the way, from wherever the two of them have been grazing, to my side; she is the one who nibbles affectionately at my hair and sleeves and settles down next to me to preen her feathers, her weight warm against my arm.

Hewlett, oh, dear Hewlett, what an injustice I have wrought against Hewlett. For the longest time I kept telling Hewlett how handsome he was getting, but he didn't seem to want to believe my sincerity; he'd keep his distance, he'd eye me disdainfully and waddle off in a huff. Then finally, when there was no trace of a question left, when those yellow-glowing white feathers were all in place and those tail feathers had no curl to them whatsoever, I had to exclaim my apology. "Hewlett, all this time I should have been telling you you were getting beautiful, not handsome!"

She eyed me with guarded hope. We were in the greenhouse, into which they'd been retiring every evening after a day of roaming the field to browse among the dandelions. They would come back to the house when it got dark, call to me to open the door, and settle into the straw, muttering to one another reassuringly whenever a cat crossed from the cat-door to the old couch. I was squatting in front of them, stroking Packard's chest—to which show of affection she responded by nibbling my hand—while Hewlett stood off behind Packard with no reason in her misunderstood self to respond to me with anything but suspicion.

"Hewlett, you're beautiful," I repeated, reaching for her slowly, and as she stood there, for the very first time allowing me to smooth the feathers on her chest, with a look on her face that made me want to cry, I was forced to notice the subtle but distinct shift in my attitude—or energy, or aura, or wherever the shift was taking place—from the way I was relating to anything male, to the way I related to anything female.

What a timely distinction it was, too, since I'd been spending time with this man whose male and female sides seemed so balanced that he was as nurturing as he was focused on his work, as sensitive to others as he was centered in his own purpose, and as openly vulnerable as he was quietly strong. I used to pride myself on regarding people as human before male or female. I was one of those mothers who enjoyed boys cuddling kittens as much as I enjoyed girls climbing trees. Now I have to look back with apology at the position into which I must have forced certain men in my life with my unconscious expectations—that they be focused, centered, and strong—while my trying to accept them as nurturing, sensitive, and vulnerable must have fallen far short of what was possible, a revelation that bowled me over when it hit home.

David was slowly revealing the layers of himself to me. Under his almost painfully shy exterior, he was creative, funny, intelligent, spiritual, tender, and competent. I was continually being pleasantly surprised by yet another facet of him. Until I met his son.

On the way to returning Daniel to his mother's house from his weekly evening visit, David stopped to drop off a video, and the first thing Daniel wanted me to know about himself, as we sat in the van, was that he had missed much of the seventh grade because he had migraines. I looked into his gentle, intelligent, reaching eyes. Being incapacitated by pounding headaches is more alarming to me than a declaration of war—external evaluations of who he was expected to be were already engaged in serious conflict with the natural glory of whom he knows himself to be—the battle was already taking its toll, inside his head.

We pulled into the driveway, and as Daniel gathered up his things, there was not so much as a word of comfort or reassurance, let alone a hug, from his father. All the way back to his place, David talked about his current project. I just didn't get it: I was in agony for his son, and he wasn't giving him a second thought.

Finally I phrased my concern as carefully as I could. "I'm sorry I'm having trouble paying attention. My mothering instincts are kicking in, and I'm wondering what can be done to help Daniel." David didn't respond, other than to start jerking his foot as he turned to his computer. Everything in me wanted to rise up in indignation at this neglectful passivity, but I held back, and as the evening progressed, I reminded myself that I had been seeing a whole lot to love in this man, a lot of which was similar to what I love in myself, but a lot of which was surprisingly and wonderfully different. I wanted to own my take on the situation, but I didn't want to assume that his should be exactly like mine. I wanted to trust that his take on it would turn out to be valid and worthy of my respect. Exhausted by my inner discipline, I fell asleep long before he was finished at the computer, but when he joined me on the mattress on his apartment floor, I woke up briefly and mumbled, "I'm sorry if I distressed you when I started talking about Daniel." His response was silence.

The next morning, out of David's earshot, I mentioned to his housemate that I'd met his son. His housemate, a woman with whom he was in a relationship following his divorce, and who recently turned to him when she was evicted from her apartment for a place to stay until she got her act together, began a tirade against his behavior concerning his son—another mama lion, as I myself have been in the past. But this time I wasn't aligning myself with a fellow crusader for children's rights. I was hurting for this man who had obviously not been granted his side of the story by his ex-wife or his ex-girlfriend. I felt protective toward him. I felt the male part of myself inwardly defending the female part of him that had been so misunderstood.

I don't even remember the words I said to him later to convey that I refused to judge him, but when I asked him if he'd ever thought about having Daniel live with him, he opened up and told me he'd always wanted that, at least during the summers, but that his having to work had made it impossible. He told me he believed Daniel needed both his father's male energy and his ability to open his third eye. He knew why Daniel was having migraines. He just couldn't see how he was going to be able to act on what he knew and wanted.

I suggested that we could include Daniel in any or all of our plans.

"That would be nice," he said quietly.

An acquired gender-oriented barrier, one of many I seem to have generated without even knowing it, dissolved, and I experienced, truly, for the first time, the premise of a wholesome man-woman relationship. It is not to bridge, overcome, or underplay the differences between a man and a woman, but simply, to use David's words, to look out for one another. I began to feel about David as if I'd rediscovered some long-lost, much-missed, early-childhood friend, a friend with whom I was fiercely and tenderly close long before there were any distinctions between male and female.

Bowled over by my revelations, I lay sprawled out on the lawn the next day. Packard came quacking toward me, and Hewlett, dear plump funny Hewlett, was right there with her, nibbling at me until I was barely able to contain myself. I wanted to screech. I've never been ticklish, but then I've never been nibbled all over from nose to toes by two ducks intent on demonstrating their uncontainable affection.

14

No More Waiting

My sister e-mailed me a message from the Hopi Nation, the main point of which is that this is not the eleventh hour, this is *the hour*—in which to speak our truth, create our community, and be good to one another. This is the time to eliminate the concept of struggle and to do everything in a sacred way. This is the time to *celebrate*. The conclusion of the message is in capital letters: "WE ARE THE ONES WE'VE BEEN WAITING FOR."

I'd put in a long, wearying day, but I hadn't attended my book study group the past two Tuesdays, having been on the West Coast, so I got back into my car, and when I turned on the ignition, the radio sang out, "Celebrate! Celebrate! Listen to the music . . ."

It was music, the inspiration that was shared by our group.

Brooke told us that during the months following her husband's suicide, she had refused to take any medication. She had preferred to meditate, to pray for protection. Every time she felt anxious or depressed, she would pray for protection. One evening, as she rearranged the logs in the fireplace, the flames leaped onto her sweater, swooshed up her sleeve, and started burning her hair. She watched, not in horror, but with the oddly calm thought, oh, no, my favorite sweater, darn, and then, oh, no, my hair, that's all I need on top of everything, frizzy hair. Meanwhile, her friend was frantically beating her with a pillow, trying to put out the flames and after a few heart-pounding moments finally succeeding in doing so. When she took stock of the damage, she was puzzled. No burnt-hair odor, no sizzled ends, nothing, her hair was fine. Her sweater was fine. "Wasn't I just on fire?" she asked her friend, who confirmed that indeed she had been, but indeed there wasn't a trace of having been so.

I was reminded of fire walking, and then of how easy it is for me to prance across my gravel driveway barefooted, when everyone else is either going oochie, ooh, ow, or wearing shoes. I had wondered why I could do this, so one day I decided to pay attention to what was happening when I walked or ran down the driveway on naked feet. I noticed that I had withdrawn myself from my feet. I was further up in my body. I wasn't connecting any of my weight to the ground. I tried consciously lowering my sense of gravity into the soles of my feet, and suddenly I was going ow, oochie, ouch. I went back up, noticing that while my physical body started at ground level, the essential me was hovering from my ankles up, and not only did I not feel any discomfort crossing the gravel, my feet didn't hurt afterwards, either. They never do.

John mentioned that he'd seen a hypnotist suggest to his subject that he was going to tickle her forearm with a feather, and then he held a lit match under her arm. She laughed, and her arm showed no signs of having been burned. Then he suggested to her that he was going to hold a lit match to her arm, and when he tickled her arm with a feather, she withdrew it with an exclamation of pain, and a blister developed on her skin.

Another member of the group recalled reading that the reason Native American shamans can shape-shift into animals is because they know they can.

It occurred to me that even though Brooke believed beings or a Being beyond herself protected her, there really isn't any difference between her belief, herself, other beings, One Being, and Reality.

I looked around at the people in the group and thought to myself, we are the ones we've been waiting for.

I wouldn't be surprised if everyone has some area in their way of being in the world that reflects this ability to self-protect, self-create, or self-shift, but that the ability comes so naturally that we hardly notice it, especially since we tend to pay so much attention to the areas that are still densely trapped within outmoded preconceptions. If we can find that area and focus on it, can we spread it into the rest of our lives? If I can walk barefooted across the sharp gravel because I take for granted that I can, because I just know I can, then I can also expect to come up with enough money to pay for my daughter's and stepdaughter's tuitions because I take for granted that I can, because I know I can. I can assume that since Fawni is drawn to becoming a massage therapist, there'll be a way for her to do so, and since Raine wants to be trained as a Waldorf teacher, she will be. I can take for granted that my relationship with David will continue to be full and rich and funny and affectionate and exciting and gratitude inspiring. I can take for granted that what I want to have happen is what *is* happening, even if it hasn't yet become evident to me.

What I wanted for my son more than anything was that he be happy, self-sovereign, and fulfilled. How could I not want that for a boy who, at the age of seven, walked in on his newborn sister and her father, his mother and grandmother, and asked, "What is this, a beauty contest? Everyone in here is so beautiful!" I told him often that I didn't care what his grades were, what other people said about him, who his friends were, or how he made his money, as long as he himself felt good about his life. There were times when I bit my tongue. He was not taking life very seriously. It was all a game to him. He was making up the rules as he went along, and they weren't exactly matched up to the rules others had decided to impose on one another. I'd ended up in the high school principal's office more than once trying to defend his follies and secretly worrying about his experiments.

But when my daughter and I visited him in Oregon recently to see what he was doing with his life, I found a master at play. Eric lives in a clean, green, fresh, culturally rich city, minutes away from hikes up to rainforest waterfalls and a wild seacoast of boulders and caves alive with purple and orange starfish and blue-green anemones. He has a roommate as easy-going as he is and a business partner who admits that he loves Eric to death. He wears his hair in a ponytail and walks the block to his office across the park in shorts, barefooted. He makes his own hours doing what he loves doing most, working with computers. He watches the sun set from the hot tub on the penthouse level of his apartment building, and he has just bought himself a BMW. He loves his life.

What impressed me the most, though, was that he welcomes into his space whoever knocks on his door, including a female friend who'd just spent five days in a mental hospital. "How was I supposed to know you can't be hanging over the side of a drawbridge that's going up, yelling and waving at the people on the boat going through underneath you?" she asked after bursting in on us.

She spilled out her story, about the handcuffs, the enforced medication, the diagnosis of bipolar disorder. She believed her mother had had something to do with her confinement. Eric's roommate, who works in a mental hospital, suggested that her mother and the other people were just trying to be helpful. "Oh, yeah, right, don't *even* go there, I'm supposed to trust *her*?" she cried out, and with the frequent use of four-letter words defined how she felt about a mother who stood by while her sister was being raped by the mother's boyfriend. As she swore and laughed and rambled and huddled in a corner of the couch, my son simply listened, with calm composure and compassion, never once giving the young woman any reason to feel judged or unwanted. She was so satisfied with the undivided attention she'd received that she was able to notice that the rest of us had been enjoying a quiet evening together, and she wanted us to continue to do so. After she'd left, Eric gently explained to his slightly befuddled roommate that all she'd needed was to be able to express herself, her pain, her ironic amusement, her frustration, not to be told how to feel, just listened to, that was all.

Not only has my son taken full responsibility for making his own life as pleasurable as suits him, he takes no responsibility whatsoever for making anyone else's life other than it is, and there is something so honest and real and open about that premise that no one feels uncomfortable around him and he feels uncomfortable around no one. At the age of twenty-six he is living in the world that I've been reaching for, one of spontaneous compassion, unlimited freedom, abundant fulfillment, and guilt-free happiness.

It wasn't too many months ago that I had read every prophecy I could find, from the Mayan calendar projection of a world shift in 2012 to Mother Shipton's description of a holocaust that few would survive. I compared the envisioned maps of the continents after the shaking up of the planet. I began to stock up on staples. But there was one message that was always tacked on to the end of every prophecy. Humanity doesn't *have* to be bludgeoned awake. We can open our eyes onto a better world for all, as easily as a child wakes up to the sound of a kitten purring in her ear. The more of us there are who take for granted that a new world is unfolding before our eyes, the more the new world makes itself visible to us.

It's already here. No need to reach. No more waiting. We already are what we've been waiting for.

15

What Do Ducks Know?

David is working on his computer in his apartment redesigning his Web site, and I'm in my house creating a new image for another print on my Adobe PhotoShop. Each of us has a phone stuck to our ear. For the last five minutes I've been listening to him breathing, with an occasional comment from his computer in the background—"I'll *never* go to the dark side!"—or in Hal's voice from *2001: A Space Odyssey,* "I'm sorry, Dave, I'm afraid I can't *do* that . . . "—and he's been listening to me occasionally remark on the effect I can create with a newly discovered tool—"Oh, duh! I can change the *pressure!*"

"This is weird, you know," I finally tell him, although I've been truly enjoying the mere presence of him. "Having nothing to say to one another, just sitting here with a phone stuck to my ear."

"Nah," he says. "It would be weird if the phone was stuck to your foot, though."

On our first "date," David took me to a rock shop so he could restock crystals for his online store. He was showing me how to tilt a crystal toward the light to look for the faint triangles on the surface that would indicate it was imbued with information, when we were interrupted by a woman exclaiming, "You're David! You did a healing on me three years ago. It was so effective! Can I have your card? I'd like to call you again."

I was putting a lot of useless effort into remaining unimpressed, so I was mildly horrified by the words that I blurted out after lunch in a Chinese restaurant. "Oh, maaan, this is when I want a cigarette the most!" He just looked at me. I shriveled. Why don't you just shut up in there, you, you, smoker, you! Here I am weighing my credentials against this man who has studied with the Masters and been visited by Mary, and you're moaning about your addiction! Duhhhmb!

We climbed into his van, and as we headed for the discount store so he could pick up some house paint, he took out a pack of cigarettes and lit one up for himself.

I stared at him in disbelief. "You lied!" I crowed with delight.

"What do you mean?"

"You said in your ad you didn't smoke."

"I didn't then."

"Oh."

"Have you been dying for a cigarette all this time?" he asked, his eyebrow arched over the grin hiding under his mustache.

"Oh, God." Oh, God, you lovely trickster, you. You've sent me a man who enjoys only an occasional glass of wine, who played with a rock band in his younger days, and who brings a pyramid he's constructed out of copper tubing to my brother's birthday picnic. Each member of my family, lying down on the grass under the pyramid, not knowing what to expect, had an instantaneous vision. My brother saw the spiral path of his life and knew what he had to do next. My sister was surrounded by loving wolves and was reminded that they mate for life. My daughter saw the colors of her chakras moving through a tunnel of light and understood that she is supposed to be bringing the light back down through her chakras in order to ground herself to the Earth. I saw a double pyramid, a diamond shape, through which appeared the face of a Light Being who seemed to want me to come back later for more information. We reported our messages with mild awe, while David nonchalantly commented, "I guess I shouldn't discontinue that size pyramid after all."

He says something to me on the phone, but because his voice is low and I have the fan on next to me, I don't catch all of his words, so I ask him to repeat what he just said. "Do you mmpher tomorr munfthig showunh or shou I rughbungleth?" is what I hear the second time, and I have to ask him, as I switch off the fan, to please say that again just one more time. This time I hear him quite clearly. "Doompher tonifrhumbul dethoobrzk ditchlgmph?"

I can *never* come back at him with a worthy retort—I'm too bowled over with incredulous gratitude. Besides, I'm giggling like a nincompoop: sometimes the messages are just as garbled as I think they are.

When I discovered how garbled the message was I thought I'd gotten from Hewlett and Packard, I could have been knocked over with a duck feather.

Packard is a male.

Packard was all brown like any respectable female mallard should be, so how was I supposed to know he'd get green feathers on his head and lovely gray ones on his back and two tail feathers that curl over his back end, just as obvious as you please?

Well, there's goes that theory. About ducks knowing anything? About me knowing anything!

So, what made Hewlett change her attitude toward me when I called her beautiful instead of handsome? Another of life's little mysteries.

You know the one about why geese fly south for the winter? That little mystery still has scientists baffled and making abashed fools out of themselves. Migration theories abound. How *do* geese, really, know how and where and why to fly when the season changes?

Well, I happen to have an answer to that one.

David was working on a roof with a buddy who also has second sight, and his buddy looked up and saw a V of Canadian geese approaching. He told David that there was a spirit leading that flock. David asked to be able to see it, and it showed itself to him as the geese flew overhead, honking. It swung back toward him and smiled at him, and then turned to continue to head the geese through the atmosphere, leaving a trail behind it, something, I imagine, like the trail of foam behind a water-skier, with its outer ridges of curling water, only this trail was a V of curling energy the geese could ride.

Then David's buddy said that if there was a disturbance in the atmosphere—and he could see there was a darkish area coming in from the west—then the next flock of geese to fly overhead would get scattered. David re-tuned his sight and saw the smoky psychic pollution floating by. And sure enough, the next V of geese, when it reached the disturbance, broke formation, and only as the scattered flock disappeared from view beyond the trees were they regathering along the energy wake of their spirit guide.

David says we can pray for guardian spirits and angels. He says when we pray for them, they hear us caring about them and thanking them, and they are much more likely to be able to show themselves to us . . . maybe because when we send them love and gratitude, we've opened our doors and crossed that threshold between belief and so-ness.

I wonder what Hewlett and Packard know that I don't.

16

Ribbon of Life

I am a small child, playing in an open, grassy park. Some-one hands me what looks like a scroll, but as I unravel it, I dis-cover it to be a long, wide, flowing ribbon of many colors. Delighted with this new plaything, I dance it into spiraling twirls, until it seems time to roll it up again and hand it back to whoever gave it to me. I turn around, but no one's there.

I notice a small open temple across the park, inside of which is sitting an ancient Asian man behind a rectangular table. His face, graced by a wispy white mustache and beard, is infinitely kind and wise. I offer the rolled-up ribbon to him, but he sim-ply sits there and gazes at me, until I understand that the col-orful ribbon is my life, and I can do with it whatever I want to.

Looking to him for approval, I unroll the ribbon across the table, letting part of it fall to the floor on either side, and then, still receiving no instructions, but heady with the power I assume has been granted me, I raise my chubby child's finger and point toward the end of the ribbon where it touches the ground to the right of the table. A beam of intent from my finger causes the ribbon to rise from the ground like a flute-enticed cobra, until it is stretched taut at an angle, attached to the right side of the temple's ceiling. I look at the old man, pleased with myself, and ask a silent question: *What now?*

What now? he asks back silently, and it occurs to me that since this is my life, I can walk it and discover what it will be like. I trot over to my left, where the ribbon is lying on the ground, and begin to walk up toward the plateau of the table, having somehow shrunk so that the ribbon has become a wide pathway, yet at the same time growing as I climb, growing gradually into an adult, encountering many people along the way, all the people I love. I cross the long flat expanse of the table, and then eagerly begin the ascent up the third of the ribbon that I've raised to the ceiling, exhilarated by the lofty feeling of aiming for the higher realms. When I finally reach the top of the ribbon, filled with a sense of ageless grandeur, I turn around for one last look at my life before lifting off.

I am horrified. All the people I've passed along the way are dead bodies strewn across the path of my life. My gut clutches at the shocking sight. This isn't right! I have to change this! I peer with impassioned intent at the dead bodies, willing the scene to change.

It refuses to be changed.

What have I done?

Suddenly the nightmarish display disappears, and I am again a child, standing before the table. I look with confusion and dismay at the ancient Asian man. His expression has not changed. He simply views me with patient wisdom, until I know what I have to do. I aim my finger at the raised end of the ribbon and undo the intention. As if released from a hook, it *falls, settling along the natural pull of gravity, its end lying on the ground to the right of the table.*

I sigh, and once again, but this time warily, I begin to walk my life. I climb, becoming an adult as I reach the plateau, and encounter again all the people I love. This time I don't eagerly walk ahead of them, this time I don't want to have to turn around from far ahead to see what has become of them. I walk with them, among them, and when I reach the edge of the table, I descend, growing older, and slowly fading, for I have given all my colors to everyone I've met, given them all the brilliant colors of the ribbon of my life, until the ribbon and I have both faded to the merest hint of pastel hues. When I reach the bottom, I turn around, and there behind me stand all my beloved friends and family, glowing, colorful, smiling happily, their arms around each other, saying thank you and good-bye. Full of peaceful joy, I bid them farewell and fade away entirely into the frayed tatters of the ribbon. A breeze strews the tatters, the breeze becomes a wind, and the wind lifts the fragments up, up toward the ceiling of the temple, and then up into the boundless sky.

In one of our hours-long conversations, encouraged by his sharing of his dreams and his encounters with spiritual beings, I described to David this vision I'd had years ago. It struck him as a parable applicable to those "traveling the path," so he asked me to type it up for his Web site, which he calls Stepping Stones . . . on the path to Light. His urging me to do so has begun the unfolding of its better half.

17

Inevitably Yours

When our book study group considered developing a spiritual center for seminars and workshops, a place was found not far away that was waiting to become exactly that. Russ, the owner of Stonehedge Gardens, hopefully and humbly welcomed us as his long-awaited assistants. Ever since his partner had died, he had wanted to expand his six acres of herb and flower gardens, lily ponds, and imported trees into a meditative retreat conducive to ecological, cultural, and spiritual awareness. With a sense of growing excitement, we laid the initial groundwork, and we spent half of our last meeting outlining some early steps to take toward our projected goal. One of the first things we needed, it was suggested, was some kind of premise or vision.

As I sat at my computer the next day, I was not intending to write a vision for the proposed center, because that would best be left to Russ. It was a vision, however, that flowed from my fingers, dictated to me by some alternate self, perhaps, or by some wiser being. Certainly it was not this present woman, who was feeling just a wee bit fearful that David, during his first visit with the group, must have found quite a few of the women exceedingly attractive. Perhaps it was some future version of myself, prompted to call back through time with some heartening words:

The awakening of humanity is as inevitable as the coming of spring, but the celestial season from which you are emerging has been so much longer than your recorded history that most of you have been laboring under the false assumption that it has not been a season at all, but the way of all time. Now, however, as you proceed along the solar system's revolution around the galaxy, you are once again, as you have been many times before, on the far edge of a shadow. You are coming into the light. It is a natural and cyclical occurrence, as certain to happen as the dawning of the sun over the Earth's horizon. You are about to open your eyes and gasp with relief that the nightmare was only that—a bad dream, a long night's despair, a long winter's struggle. You are about to look around at one another and see the comforting faces of your family as you share the abundance of your prospects. You are about to experience, as if for the first time, what your race has almost forgotten—the balmy climate of opened hearts, freedom, excitement, peacefulness, and bliss.

The dawning of this celestial spring is upon you: you can neither make it happen nor stop it from happening. Why then do some of you feel compelled to ensure that it does? If that is what you do feel, compelled to make it happen, then you are still dreaming, for if you were awake, you would be compelled only to nudge those next to you out of the bad dreams within which they are crying, and, with your arms around them, point to the dawn. You would simply want to tell the winterbound souls who are despairing of ever being warm again, well-fed again, to notice that they are still alive, and that under the thinning ice the rivers are flowing, under the melting snow the grasses are growing.

As you begin to comprehend what is being heralded by the light glowing on the horizon, you will shake off the illusions of your restless slumber and gaze in awe at the heretofore unseen world around you. You will remember how real the dream seemed—even in your lucid moments, which you called second sight, you'd forgotten what you are experiencing now—true sight. As you shake off the protective garments worn against the bitterness, you will remember how heavy you thought you'd always been and would be, and you will rejoice in levity. You thought you were doomed by waning supplies. Surprise! You thought you would never outlive your unmet needs, your secret greeds, and your isolation. But you will look around and see your loved ones, casting off their coats of armor, reaching for your hands, planning your new garden.

Be assured, you will not die in your sleep of hunger or cold. The day has come; the new season is here. You can share your winter-long dreams if you need to, or forget them, if they were painful, or use them, if they were inspiring, or you can simply be awake and fresh, in this reality where miracles are natural, where you truly see one another, where you are profusely and abundantly in love with Life.

I leaned back in my chair and pondered this message. If we are co-creators with the Source of Light, if we create our own realities, if thoughts are so powerful that thinking makes it so, if this is one possible future that we can assume to be attainable and intend to reach, if we cast a lifeline from this, our present reality, toward that one, and pull ourselves forward convinced of its truth, could it indeed become truth?

I shared it with the members of my book study group by passing out copies, explaining that it wasn't meant to be part of our Stonehedge project, although I hoped it might help trigger a sense of mission. John asked if he could read it out loud. As he did, a calm descended on our little group. No one spoke when he was finished. Several people had a vaguely smiling, faraway look in their eyes. Lynn, however, was ready to move on to more mundane matters. As was I, when I got home.

I e-mailed the message to David, but I asked him not to read it, at least not until he'd responded to the part of my e-mail in which I told him that I don't mind if he finds other women attractive, which seems only natural, but is he with me only because he thinks I'm part of his spiritual purpose?

He doesn't e-mail me back. I check three times. Finally I shut down my computer, and the minute I do, the phone rings.

"Do you think I would trade you in for anyone else?" he asks.

My heart does a cartwheel, and my reading glasses go flying. I'll have to retrieve them later, of course, or I wouldn't be able to decipher how many cups of water to add to the rice I'm going to fix him for dinner one day. (I haven't cooked since Fawni began to spoil me with her superb gourmet creations two years ago. Eleven years of being a short-order cook to five different teenage appetites burned out what miniscule interest I once had in making actual *meals*. Poking around in the refrigerator for that corner of cheese that hasn't turned to fissured rubber yet totally satisfies the annoying necessity of supplying *my* body with nutrients.) David is well aware of my abhorrence of the kitchen. And still he wouldn't trade me in? Wake up and smell the spring!

Is this what it looks like, the new day? The same as always? Only different?

It is said that before enlightenment, a tree is just a tree. During enlightenment, a tree is not just a tree. After enlightenment, a tree is a tree. Before enlightenment, the world is just the world. During enlightenment, the world is not just the world. After enlightenment, the world is the world. It's not going to look all that different. And it's going to look so different. And this is just the beginning of how much the same and how different it's going to look.

18

Looking Forward

When was there ever a time, in all of recorded history, that in large areas of the world, during a witheringly hot season, most of the inhabitants worked, lived, or could visit somewhere that had cool, fresh air-conditioning? Not during the Crusades, not during the French Revolution, not during the Civil War, not during the advance across North America, not during World War II. They sweated it out.

Every time David and I stepped out of my air-conditioned car yesterday, into a hundred and two degrees of sweltering humidity, I would tell myself this is just like a sauna; people pay to clean out their toxins this way and we're getting it for free. Nevertheless, in the office furniture stores we visited, we both tried out every one of the office chairs, prolonging our decision as we cooled down from groggy and soggy to cheery and clear. "What do you think?" "I think we should check out another place." "Yeah." We each comfort-tested about ninety-seven office chairs. Neither one of us has air-conditioning at home.

But I do have a long garden hose. Funny how people will run from your good intentions when you're laughing wickedly.

Looking forward (as an idealist I tend to look back to see what I can appreciate about the present, and to look forward—really look forward—to what the present can become), my brother told me about an encounter that left him astounded.

A woman and her ten-year-old son were visiting my brother Val, who gives tours of his "eco-path," a trail through the woods embellished with his whimsical, thought-provoking metal sculptures. As they stood talking on the lawn, the boy told him, "I have magical powers."

"Oh, well, that's wonderful," my brother responded, not knowing how patronizing he must have sounded. The boy turned around, faced the trees, and then proceeded to raise his arms from his side, very slowly, bringing them up to a horizontal level as he gradually lifted himself up into the air, about three or four inches off the ground. My brother chuckled. "Hey, that's a good trick!" He couldn't make sense of being able to see the grass under the boy's feet.

The boy came down, turned around, and looked at my brother, sighingly aware that Val had not grasped what he'd witnessed. So he did it again—slowly lifted himself off the ground. Val was now laughing and frowning at the same time, utterly bewildered. The boy did it a third time, raising his arms and gradually lifting himself a few inches into the air. As Val comprehended the shadow, the grass, the space, and the feet suspended at an angle, he noticed that the boy's mother, although she appreciated the effect on Val, was herself not in the least mystified, having learned to take her son's ability to levitate for granted.

I just learned how to doggie paddle through the humidity and some ten-year-old kid comes along and swan dives into the air.

I love it.

19

Take Down the Ladders

There was one variable I forgot about when Hewlett let me pet her for the first time in the greenhouse. David was present. David's presence in my life has aligned me with the sweet mysterious wonder of everything.

Apparently my presence has helped align him as well. For over fifteen years he's been supporting himself with home-improvement-type work. To put to good use his other gifts and talents, he began developing his Web site in his spare time two years ago. And last week he finally decided he could no longer afford the time and energy for house painting and carpentry. Although he didn't know where the money would come from, he took the ladders down off his van. Within days he was getting enough orders for healing tools and New Age CD's, and

enough requests for guidance and healing, to begin to believe that the change he's wanted is truly happening. He attributes it to having resubmitted his Web site to the search engine with a new domain name. He may be right, but I also think he's resubmitted his intention to the universe, which said, "Ah so, no more mixed messages; what you want is now clear enough to respond to, thank you very much, and you're very welcome."

Meanwhile, back in the old world, David's ex-girlfriend Angel (not her real name) has been "temporarily" parked in his apartment for what has lengthened into five months now. He assumed originally that although he doesn't mind providing a haven for her, if he maintained nothing more evident than a tolerance for the situation, she'd eventually find her own direction and follow it, but it has become apparent that she isn't moving on because she can't move on. She doesn't have a car or a job or anyone to move in with. She is an unshielded human being; the psychic pollution in the atmosphere is too much for her to handle; she is exceedingly intelligent, tormented, perceptive, funny, lonely, and desperate; and she is here, in our lives.

No past lessons apply.

Two years ago, my then-husband leaped into the back of the pickup truck I was using to escape his rage, and shoved a four-by-four through the back window, splintering glass everywhere as it grazed my ear on its way to smashing into the dashboard. Later, when he demanded that I come to him for a hug, I said from the doorway of the bedroom, "I can't do that."

"Well, then, I'm going to have to kill you," he told me.

I walked over to the side of the bed where he was resting, picked up the knife he kept on the nightstand, and handed it to him. "Well, then, I guess you'd better get it over with," I told him.

He smiled and shook his head at me as if I was so clueless. "That's not the knife I'm going to use," he informed me.

I left.

I called him from my hiding place a few days later and told him he had to move out of my house or he would never see me again. I knew he could move in with his parents, and as it turned out, they needed him—his father, the only driver, was losing his eyesight.

Based on that experience, I figured it was our responsibility to close a door for Angel so she would look for an open one to walk through. But there are no open doors, none that we can see, and while it may be that one will open when the time is right, for now, Angel is here, and she most certainly is not attacking us; she is merely depending on David's good will for a place to live.

I asked for wisdom.

Do unto others as you would have the universe do unto you, was the response to my request.

I would have wanted the universe to stop me from acting the way my ex-husband was acting.

What would I want from the universe if I were Angel?

David and I, having agreed on the answer, told her that whatever kind of help she wanted from us, we wanted to offer it. If she wanted help moving on, we would help her. If she wanted to stay, she was welcome to stay, and if she thought she needed us, she should remember that we need her, too.

I didn't even know that last part was true until the words came out of my mouth. Why else would she be here if it wasn't a mutual gift?

I asked David if it was possible for Angel to be healed from being so unshielded. He said that he had tried to channel healing for her in the past, but she would have to want to be whole for the healing to last. Then he reconsidered—no past lessons apply—and he shrugged. "Anything's possible."

Which is why, it seems to me, we need her in our lives. To remind us that anything is possible. Living with an ex-girlfriend is not only possible, it's the best way to live when there is no other way to live and still feel good about Life.

If there is a better way, please, Whoever's Up There, let us know what it is.

Meanwhile, we're taking the ladders down. Not trying to climb up and out of here.

Taking the ladders down. Doing what feels good to do.

Do unto others as if you were the universe, because, in fact, you are, and so are they.

20

Gifts

Eleven years ago, on my forty-fourth birthday, as I lay down to fall asleep, I found myself in a large round room, in the center of which was a large oval table. I sat down in one of the thirteen chairs and noticed that there were thirteen doors in the circular wall.

One of them opened. A Being of Light came through it, approached me, gave me a gift, and then sat at the table. After I had contemplated the gift, a second door opened, and a second Being of Light brought me another gift.

This went on, every few days or weeks for the next few months, until I had received eleven gifts, and eleven Beings of Light sat around the table, and eleven doors stood open to the Light from whence they'd come, with two still closed.

I didn't know why there were still two doors closed, although it seemed that one was waiting for the twelfth Being to open it from the outside, and one was meant for me to open outward once I had learned to appreciate and develop each gift.

I haven't mastered the gifts yet. Actually, I'm still trying to understand them.

The first gift was paradox: the ability to shift one's perspective so that all truths, even apparently opposing or mutually exclusive ones, are encompassed within the one truth. The ability to say *and* rather than *either*. Or *all of the above*. Yielding to the Mystery, or admitting that living in a three-dimensional perspective has its limitations.

If we lived in a two-dimensional reality and we wanted to experience a three-dimensional tree, we could only slide our flat perspective through time and deduce from the sequential cross sections what the tree would look like in three dimensions. The cross section of the trunk would appear to be a large uneven circle. As we slid our perspective, like a piece of paper, higher, the circle would appear to separate into smaller circles that would appear to wander in relationship to one another as they diminished in diameter and broke off into even smaller circles. Finally we would see scattered, disconnected, odd shapes, and it would take a leap in perspective to understand how the leaves were connected to the trunk.

So, with our three-dimensional perspective, we need to make a leap to understand how everything is connected and relative and explainable and all part of the bigger picture of more dimensions that exist all at once. If you could move your perspective outside of the solar system and into that of a four-dimensional being, the Earth's journey through time would appear to be a solidly coiled spiral around the sun, which would appear to be a long curving rod spiraling around the center of the galaxy as the galaxy moved through space.

Each fraction of a second of your three-dimensional perception is really only a cross section of a solid Earth-in-time, or of mankind-through-time, or of your lifespan, all of which exist from beginning to end all at once, just as the tree's trunk, its origin, and its leaves, all of its possible outcomes, exist at the same time. Clairvoyance and time travel and communicating with those who no longer have bodies would be no more paradoxical to a four-dimensional perspective than a blue jay chirping to and landing next to another blue jay on another branch of the tree.

If we slid our two-dimensional cross section of the tree up far enough, we'd come to where the tree seemed to disappear altogether. It would seem to have stopped existing. We would think of it as having once existed as disconnected circles but now that time is past. Until we slid our perspective down again and discovered the tree to be giving birth to itself in odd disconnected shapes that grew into small circles that all crowded together, in time, into one large circle. To say that the small circles existed at the same time as the large circle would be like us three-dimensional viewers saying that the child and the man exist at the same time, or like saying up and down are aspects of the same thing. Going back in time and changing something would change everything. And it wouldn't. Because everything is big enough to accommodate all possible and probable realities at once, including nothing.

Paradox is simply not seeing the continuum within which everything is the same thing, even though it's not. Or, as David's friend Dan put it, "It all boils down to everything being both discrete and continuous. I am individuated," he explained, "and I'm not—I'm also connected to everything. You remember that kid's question? If God can do anything, can He make a rock that's so heavy He can't lift it? Well, see, God's answer to that is Yes, I am that powerful, *and* No, I'm not."

Okay, I think I have a handle on that one.

Now all I have to do is learn how to shift my perspective, like that ten-year-old boy did when he levitated in front of my brother, so that gravity and no gravity are the same thing, so that physical laws exist at the same time that they don't. The more I think about it, the more I see how paradox could be quite the handy gift.

The second gift was guidance. The ability to draw to oneself that which can be interpreted as communication with Spirit.

Several years ago I spent a week alone at the sacred monument known to the Navajo as Rock with Wings. I was on the verge of telling Whoever's Up There to get me off this planet, this stinks, I'm lost, I quit. But I was out in the middle of the desert, and there weren't any booths from which to phone home, so I figured I'd have to create my own version of smoke signals in reverse. You Up There, I'm going to use my soul symbol, an eight-pointed star within a diamond (which was what I saw when I looked through my third eye) as my calling card—so You can get through to me. (I had a bit of an attitude.)

I painted an eight-pointed star on one side of a small diamond-shaped stone, and on the other side I painted a woman in a sarcophagus. Give me my soul or give me death. Please.

I climbed up the incline to the base of Rock with Wings. Inside a small cave, I left the diamond-shaped stone propped at an angle against the base of one wall, coffin-side up: I surrender my soul into Your keeping.

As I left, I brushed away my tracks from the sandy entrance to the cave, in reverence for the sacred nature of this powerful place.

When I returned to the Rock that night, after having taken a day trip to Chaco Canyon, I felt drawn to return to the small cave, which I did the next morning. I stopped at the entrance, somewhat stunned, staring at what I saw on the sandy ground. Formed with two obtuse-angled twigs facing one another and touching at their ends, was the shape of a diamond, and inside the diamond was a right-angled twig, placed to look like the letter L—my initial.

How did that get there?

I checked the ground for tracks.

No tracks.

No mouse tracks or bird tracks or any tracks at all.

Just three carefully placed twigs in the shape of a diamond enclosing my initial.

A feeling of being observed came over me, of being cared about, communicated with.

I looked up at the towering Rock in awe.

Then I ducked into the cave, and there was my diamond-shaped stone, but not as I had left it, coffin-side up. It was still in the same place, at the base of the wall, but it had been turned over. It was star-side up.

My plea had been answered.

I'd been guided to reclaim my soul.

I began to listen and watch for guidance.

I've done a serious amount of stumbling since then. I still haven't mastered how to read what form guidance comes in. Either that or I was supposed to take exactly the route I did to get here. Oops. Either, or? No, Lesta, try *and*. I still don't always know how to interpret guidance *and* apparently I do, because here I am. And even though I like it here, I'm bound to be moving into what looks like there from here, so I'm glad I have that gift of guidance.

Thank you, Whoever You Are.

The third gift was called culmination and source. In a kind of holographic block of information, I was given to understand that while I am the sum of all my experiences, my genetic inheritance, my soul's past lives, my culture's history, and everything that has contributed to the unique I that I am, I am also the starting point of everything that will be influenced by me: my children, my environment, my culture, my future lives. I have been created from stardust and from generations upon generations of ancestors beginning with amino acids. I have been created from experiences so infinitely numerous I can't even remember a fraction of them. I am the culmination of all that has funneled itself into me, and although I feel like the narrow part of an hourglass, what I am doing and being in my own little way and little space is the source of a spreading forth of unaccountable changes: the ways in which I touch people who will be moved to touch others; the things I teach my children that they will improve upon as they teach theirs; the work that I do that will affect the world in ways I will never see. I am the middle point in a vortex that has no beginning and no end.

No wonder I'm stressed!

This is a gift? This is a major exercise in appreciation and responsibility!

No wonder I'm such a tangled mess of multidimensional conflicts. No wonder I'm such a miracle of unique qualities. No wonder I want to be unconscious of the consequences of my actions. No wonder I want to act carefully.

But maybe, too, there is no need for me to know exactly what the outcome of my actions will be, only that there will be outcomes far beyond my personal reach. When my grandfather bought a painting from an artist who needed the money, because he liked it, because he cared, how could he have known that when it got passed on to me and I sold it, there would be money enough for my stepdaughter to get accredited as a Waldorf school teacher, and for my daughter to become accredited as a massage therapist? Did he have any idea that just when I would be developing an understanding of how my loving intentions could attract their manifestation, his act would become the means through which the universe could provide substantial evidence? Did he foresee how many students will be encouraged and inspired, how many clients refreshed into a new take on life, how many people's lives would be enhanced by that one seemingly insignificant but caring act of his?

Thank you, everything that came before me and created me. I want to pass it on, everything I can, with gratitude and love.

The fourth gift is noticing that I am a reflection of the One.

I was given a cassette tape recorded by my friend Jacque, on which she reads her poems over a background of angelic chants and ethereal music. As her work of art reaches its uplifting crescendo, she speaks, in a voice that could belong to the Goddess herself, for the universe: I . . . Am. We . . . Are. This . . . Is . . . Me.

Listening to the cassette as I was driving around on various errands, those words, repeated slowly as the music grew more and more buoyant, made me look at everything as if I had created it, and in doing so, had discovered what was beautiful about myself.

That tree: this . . . is . . . me. Oh, my, then I am reaching for the sky, I am shading those beneath me, I am breathing oxygen into the atmosphere, and I am swaying in the breeze. How can I not love myself for being a tree?

That grizzled, tattered, hunched old man, rooting through the trash: this . . . is . . . me. Then I am lonely, an outcast, living from hand to mouth, unable to bathe, making people feel ashamed and grateful, humming to myself, dying inside. Oh, precious part of me, how can I not love myself in you?

That decrepit building: this is me. I was built by men with dreams, men with families, tired men, inspired men, to shut out the sky and the cold and the insects, to box in and protect. I stand as a marker in the history of struggle and achievement, of brilliance and ignorance, of the crumbling of old ways before the new. How can I not be in awe of how many lives I have witnessed and influenced? How can I not feel affection for the symbol I am of human endeavor and foolishness?

That teenager leaning against a signpost, bopping her shoulders to the music pumping from the radio on the stoop, exhaling the smoke of a cigarette, tossing the beaded black braids out of her eyes, bending over double laughing at what her friend just said, stubbing out her cigarette with her purple sneaker, how can I not love her audacity and carelessness and courage? She is me, not knowing what her future holds, getting what she can from what she has.

That rose, opening its delicately blushing petals, wafting its fragrance into the fumes of passing cars, attracting a butterfly into the sweetness of its secrets—that incongruous rose is me, my gift to myself of remembrance. I Am. We Are. We are the reflection, the mirror, the image, the Self that wants to know Itself in every possible way.

Well, tomorrow is going to be another full day, so I'm outta here.

Catch you later . . . you who are such a wonderful paradox, being guided by Spirit even as you use your own free will, you who are the unique culmination and the unique source of infinite influences, you who are creation and Creator.

21

Gifts in Action

Because David has been spending more time at my place, having set up an office in which we can work side-by-side on the Web site and incoming orders and outgoing information, we've just been stopping in at his place every other day or so for the past week to check the mail and to make sure that Angel has everything she needs.

Yesterday's visit was a little unsettling. She described nightly visits from intruders that had left her sleepless and ragged. She accused me, glancing at David, of taking away her protector. She narrowed her eyes at me. "Don't even pretend to be my friend!" She also said, however, with another glance at David, "Lesta, it's not your problem."

Each bitter remark was punctuated with that observation,

and although I was inclined to assume that it was meant ironically, it also sounded like the one true message being given to me by her higher self. I ended the conversation with, "Do you need anything while we're here? Milk, cigarettes?" She checked and said no, she had enough of everything. But she was still bristling.

I was rattled.

If I'd decided to accept a rattlesnake living in my back yard, and I gave it plenty of room, but one day it quivered the tip of its tail at me, I would have felt the same way. Okay, it's not really my back yard; I'm just living on this plot of land, too, but hey.

So what do I do? I picture myself staying clear of Angel altogether, thinking one warning's all I need. I'm not into poison.

I picture myself asking her, the next time she describes male intruders making loud noises downstairs, even though the doors are still locked the next morning, "Who raped you?" I believe her terrible fears have taken on a life of their own, and I wish I could relieve her, help her become a witness to her own part in materializing what she dreads the most, help her, not to step outside of the fear and look at it from a safe place, because there is no safe place outside of it, but to step into its arena, converse with it, give it its proper perspective . . . But I don't know—this is a case of the power of a lifetime of caged, denied, neglected, deformed, and ultimately monstrous fear pitted against the power of one of the gifts I received eleven years ago.

Gift number five: the power of peace. The ability to maintain purity, wholeness, inspiration, and balance. The ability to align with Spirit, to become a channel for serenity and acceptance. The ability to be a transformer of stress-producing emotions into life-enhancing emotions, to flow outward, to include everything within the limitlessness of love, to trust, to know, and to remind that all is just as it needs to be.

This is testing time. Spirit has sent me a challenge to see if

I have mastered this gift. Geez. I haven't mastered any of them. How am I supposed to know which gift to use when?

Because gift number six is an intelligent aura. I have been given the ability to filter out what I don't need, to receive what I do need, to draw in what is healthy and growth-enhancing, to repel what isn't, and to send forth what is beneficial to those around me. This gift of automatically impeccable sensitivity, if I can learn to make good use of it, eliminates helplessness and solves problems without my having to use my mind to sort through possible outcomes. In other words, I don't even have to picture what I might do at some point in the future. All I have to do is trust that I will do the right thing at the right time without even trying.

I'm about to write "easier said than done," when in walks David's friend Dan, who proceeds to tell us that he has been taking Angel out to eat and to do her laundry, and that even though she's upset by our increased absence, he sees it as a necessary and good change. He believes that she is coming to grips with what she needs to do next, which is to find someone to share a place with her, since living alone is becoming unbearable. He recommends that we stay away as much as possible to let this decision substantiate itself. He believes in tough love, and he believes she is capable of summoning the strength to make a move. His words sound like a blessing to me, wisdom offered from an even greater place of compassion than my own. I am being reminded that guidance is the ability to draw to myself that which can be interpreted as communication with Spirit, and I am being released to act within the context of gift number seven.

Self-evident purpose. The ability to have total trust in the alignment of my individual purpose with the greater purpose. Whatever I have done, whatever I am doing, and whatever I will do is all preparation, enactment, and fulfillment of my reason for being here. I'm here for many reasons: to experience, to learn, to create, to be in love with life, to teach, to be human, to be divinely inspired, to open myself, to expand, to contract, to breathe, to whisper, to play, to dream, to make known what is secret, to bless and be blessed.

One of the things that Dan said in our conversation was that a healthy life, as simply as he could determine it, is one with no regrets.

I have regrets. When I was called into the high school principal's office and was handed a letter that had been taken from my daughter's locker during a search for drugs, I *wish* I hadn't unfolded it and read it and swallowed my reactions and waited until my daughter and I were outside of the school building before hugging her. I wish I'd kept the letter folded and asked the principal if he had my daughter's permission to read it. I wish I'd told him that suspending a straight-A student for something she'd disclosed to a friend that had happened the previous summer was *incredibly stupid*.

The downside of the forgetfulness that so intriguingly wraps the present of life's mystery is finding *myself* acting as if I'm incredibly stupid. But the upside of regrets is that they trigger remembrance. Oh, the way I *could* have acted, had I understood my gift of self-evident purpose, had I been as unintimidated, as uncalculated as a child or a tree or the wind, had I simply pointed out the obvious and been true to my daughter and myself.

Until I am beyond listing my reasons for being here, and beyond having to forgive myself for my chosen forgetfulness, I will not be making the best use of this gift.

22

Family Surprises

Hewlett and Packard didn't quite know what to make of us when we backed our vehicles up to their mini-pond, used the hose that runs fresh water into it, and, after sponging and rinsing off our vans, ran around the yard like idiots, yelling and screaming. David's son Daniel, with an expertise even hours of video games couldn't account for, wielded the nozzle like a bonafide warrior, keeping both his drenched father and me on the other side of the driveway, just out of reach of the downpour. Bellowing like a blue-faced Braveheart into the battle, I dashed toward the pond, grabbed the hose and ha! kinked it. "Run, David, run!" I shouted as Daniel's weapon drizzled to a drip, and like the cinematic character Forrest Gump, David turned into a running fool and hightailed it for the front door. In order to follow suit, I had to let go of the hose.

When Daniel joined us in the living room and viewed the results of his sharp shooting—his father's hair flattened, bare feet leaving puddles on the floor, and my shirt sopping wet—he raised his fist and grinned: "Victory!" I came out of the kitchen holding a cup of water and Daniel took off down the hall, out of reach of the arc of liquid aimed at him. "Victory in attack *and* evasion!" I conceded loudly, not mentioning that at least David and I were now pleasantly cooled off enough to endure this second wave of hundred-degree weather.

Despite their earlier concern about the trustworthiness of unduly excitable humans, Hewlett and Packard came quacking up to me later as I stroked the kittens, jealously lunging at them with harmless beaks, and nibbled at me with so much delight (because I was wet?) that Hewlett even let me pick her up and hold her. She didn't squirm at all, she just calmly and somewhat proudly settled into my arms, her yellow-tinted white feathers smooth against my skin, while Packard tilted his lovely blue-green head up at us in unusual silence.

Every day is full of surprises.

The eighth gift was astral travel.

I've made use of that gift out of curiosity on several occasions. Once I spirited myself to the house of someone I'd never visited in person and later discovered that it was indeed laid out the way I'd seen it. Once I rose above the planet at such speed that I didn't have time to look back and see my body. What I saw instead by the time I did look back was a long hollow cable, coiling downwards and disappearing into the atmosphere beneath me. Inside it were what seemed to be organic pages, like the underside of a mushroom, pages on which were recorded countless lifetimes. They seemed to be my soul's Akashic records.

I've made use of this gift to visit the limitlessness of being. Instead of perceiving as a single point of consciousness, I found myself perceiving as a sphere that was expanding in all directions at once, at first at the speed of light, until I realized it would take me four years for the periphery of my awareness to encounter the nearest star beyond the sun, and then at the speed of thought, encompassing infinite numbers of tiny clusters of galaxies in seconds. Suddenly I broke the envelope and burst into the now of everywhere, which is no speed at all, but all and nothing all at once—the most exquisite fullness and emptiness of being, all-knowing, unknowing, blissful, peaceful Light.

But the best use I made of that gift was during the years that five children were sleeping under my roof, in various stages of comfort and restlessness, of security and anxiety. I would lie in my bed, rise out of myself, hover above the house, and sprinkle handfuls of golden stardust over them, sending them protection and love. It would feel so good to do that, that I would rise higher and cast stardust over the whole valley, and then over the houses of all the people I loved, even those who lived in different states.

Finally I rose high enough to sprinkle stardust energy over the whole planet. As I was doing that, sending peace and love to everyone on the planet, I saw that I was not the only one. There were many astral bodies glowing in the dark of space just above the atmosphere, a whole interwoven network of beings I did not know, creating a light-grid of beautiful prayers all around the Earth.

The ninth gift was memory of past and future, of all pasts and all futures. I think I experienced that memory when I exploded out of myself into infinity and eternity, but I don't remember. Maybe I don't have to. Maybe just knowing that all pasts and all futures exist now is enough to give me the perspective I need in this little life of mine.

The tenth was lucid dreaming. The ability to know when I am dreaming. The ability to recognize this little self called Lesta as a character in one of my dreams.

The eleventh was happiness. I was happy to get that one, but I didn't really know that it was more than just an occasional present to be opened and enjoyed, that it was a maintainable state of being, until just a few months ago, until almost eleven years after I was made aware that it was my present to enjoy constantly.

After I'd received those eleven gifts over the period of a few months following my forty-fourth birthday, there were no more.

I mentioned this to my then eight-year-old daughter, the discrepancy between the number of doors through which the Light Beings had entered the circular room, and the number of gifts, which I described to her.

One afternoon soon after that, Fawni said to me, "Mom," or maybe she said Modu, or Mommasopolis, or Produce (as in groceries), or one of the many other names she had for me at the time, "I'm going to give you your twelfth gift now."

My eyebrows went up.

She drew a picture for me. "It's the Fountain of Youth," she said, smiling at me wisely as she handed it to me. "You can be any age you want to be."

Discovering that one of the members of your Light Being family is living in your house with you is likely to flip you out. And then flip you back in again with a whole new take on things. You begin to look around and wonder if you've been missing something. That light coming out of your son's eyes as he gives you yet another profoundly wise word of advice. That weird paradoxical sense of humor your brother has. That calming, peaceful tone in your sister's voice. . . .

The Fountain of Youth. The freedom to get down on my hands and knees, when my four-year-old daughter is telling me to go make some popcorn, to crawl over to her and whine, "But I don't wanna make the pockorn, Mommy, *you* make it!" and to scoot away before she can clobber me with her teddy bear. Or to beg my five-year-old son, "Play wif me," only to have him tell me, "No! Go find something to do by yourself, I'm too busy!" The freedom to be an adolescent, in love for the first time. To be on my deathbed, looking back at my life, and saying, "Yes!" To be thirty thousand years old, at peace with the perishability and renewal that is life. To be ageless, in love with All Time.

Daniel, contented (headache-free since summer vacation began), settled down in front of his video game, and David, having changed into dry clothes, settled down in front of his computer. After feeding Fawni's fish, which she'd asked me to do until she returned from a four-day trip, I went into her massage room and lay down under David's Atlantean pyramid, thinking about my family of Light Beings. Maybe it was because the guys were so absorbed in their own activities, or maybe it was because I'd been writing about the gifts—I found myself missing that family, wondering if they would ever spend time with me again. I was actually lonely for the first time in months.

I heard a car in the driveway, and then a door shut, and then voices in the living room. When I went out to see who was here, there was one of the members of my Light Being family.

My daughter had come home a day early.

23

Don't Wake Me till It's Over

Lucid dreaming—there's more to it than just realizing that I am a character in one of my soul's dreams.

It could be the answer to why that ten-year-old boy could levitate in the face of my brother's incredulity. It could be the answer to why someone can bend a spoon by looking at it, or heal cancer, or materialize an orange in his hand, or lift a truck off her child.

It could be the answer to why one person can commit a crime against society's rules and not get caught, and another can try to get away with something illegal and be made to answer for it—or why some people's lives end in disaster and others in glory.

We are all participating in one big dream.

The ancients of many cultures have tried to tell us so.

But, as I'm understanding it now, it's not a dream in which we've all *agreed* to a general background of physical laws, constancy of seasons, solidity of rocks, movement of time from birth to death. As I see it now, there are more of us participating in this dream than I thought. The Earth's dream includes her revolution around the sun; the rock's dream includes its slow evolution from breaking off a cliff to being tumbled in the waves. Some people die of old age by the time they're twelve, while others still look sixty when they're a hundred and twenty. Some people are colorblind, and others see auras.

Everything that has form is dreaming its form in its own way, at its own pace. If we experience a general constancy, it's because we are dreaming among other forms dreaming a constancy to which we can relate. Meanwhile, there are beings who are dreaming at a much more rapid frequency, so most of us don't notice them flitting through our dream-reality, and dream-beings who are so tiny or so immense that they are beyond the spectrum of our dream-perception. We generally overlap our dreams with others that create a sense of continuity and prevent us from getting overloaded so we can focus on the reason we're having this particular dream.

When that boy levitated, he was still dreaming—he is still visible and tangible to himself in his dream—but he knows it's a dream. When we know we're dreaming, we can do whatever we want to: We can fly, we can shift scenes instantly, we can reflect our needs and fears and wishes to ourselves, we can see into other places and times.

Those who are lucid dreaming can work miracles, manipulate matter, dodge disaster, or appear in two places at once, because they don't buy into the rules created by ignorance or habit or unconsciousness. The miracles they work only seem to be miracles because they are outside of the artificial rules others have bought into. Yet it is outside of the rules where true reality—the fullest, freest expression of divine potential—exists.

When I was nineteen, I dreamed I was following two of my college friends across a railroad track in view of an oncoming train. They made it, but I didn't. The train killed me. Wait a minute, I said to myself in the dream: This is my dream, why am I killing myself? So I dreamed a retake. I jumped across the tracks just in time, and the train whizzed by behind me. Interestingly, the time factor of the retake was part of the time sequence of the dream, so when I found myself on the other side of the tracks, safe and sound, my two friends, who had gone on, were no longer in sight. I woke up so excited. I had just had my first lucid dream. I had just told myself that I could avoid the impact of whatever powerful forces were about to intersect my path and determine a different outcome for myself. A few months later, not conscious at the time that I was acting on that dream, I transferred to another school, and opened up a whole new life for myself.

I don't want to jolt myself awake from this dream by crashing into a supposedly solid wall, but I wonder, would I wake up fully and die to this life-dream if I were suddenly able to walk *through* what looks and feels like a solid wall? Hmm. If I could walk through walls, maybe I wouldn't wake up and die, but maybe, with the dream that evident, I would have a hard time relating to anyone pounding on the wall. I'd end up kinda lonely. Even my kids would be way too much in awe of me.

For now, I just want to bend my dream in a way that isn't too far ahead of my ability to assimilate it. The rules I want to dismiss from my dream aren't the ones that keep mountains in their places, not yet, anyway, even though a lucid dreamer has told us that we *can* move mountains. The rules I want to dismiss from my dream are just the ones that have limited my perception of what's possible in order to maintain my love of life, my sweet dream, until I'm ready to wake up.

One winter day, twenty-two years ago, with my four-year-old son beside me, I drove my pickup truck down a short steep hill toward an intersection. I stepped on the brakes and heart-poundingly realized that the road was covered with ice all the way to the bottom. I tried to brake in short spurts, but the tires were sliding and the weight of the truck was building a momentum. We were about to slide right through the red light into moving traffic, and there was no telling how much control the passing drivers had over their own vehicles, even if I laid on the horn and warned them. An accident was imminent. In what felt like a moment of intense and yet calm power, I willed the truck to stop. Without thinking or feeling, I used all of my intent to bring that truck to a stop before it reached the traffic light. It stopped.

When my moment of pure, calm intent gave way to a trembling aftershock, I found my foot pressing the brake to the floor, and my arms pulling the steering wheel practically out of its socket, but neither of those unconscious physical acts had counter-acted the sheet of ice beneath my vehicle. I simply wasn't ready to wake up from this life-dream of mine; I didn't want to force my son to wake up from his; and I didn't want the dream to be about healing broken bodies—so I became a lucid dreamer and changed the course of action. Just as I've found myself falling in a dream and at the last second swooping up and flying, I had known how to keep myself from waking up.

This means I don't have to die until I'm ready to. I like this dream. I don't want to wake up yet. But when I do wake up— I wonder—is something about this life of mine, this dream, going to be an exciting message for the awake me who is momentarily dreaming? When I have a dream, I wake up knowing something more about myself, about my choices or how someone else is really affecting me or what inspiration I want to act on next. So when the dreamer who is dreaming this life wakes up, is she going to have gained something from it? Am I going to have given her some information she hasn't yet brought into her awareness? Am I her subconscious mind, giving her messages, symbols to interpret, clues to who she really is and what she's doing on her grander scale?

I love remembering my dreams. I want her to love remembering this one.

I have to say, though, I love the nightmares as well. They give me a great deal. When I was beginning to sense that I wouldn't be staying with my daughter's father, I shrank from deciding to initiate such a potentially devastating change, from the pain I believed I was going to cause. Then one night I dreamed that a sinister motorcyclist with a shaved head, wearing black leather clothes and heavy boots, stomped on my daughter and shot her father, and then imprisoned me in a house that refused to be changed. It was my mother's house. When I tried to move the furniture, it would move itself back. *Who are you?* I asked the assassin in horror. *I am the part of you that would kill and maim to remain the same,* I was told. Wow. What a switch on my conscious take of the situation. One of my subconscious selves had given me a vivid illustration of my fear's twisted power. I thanked my assassin and no longer feared the changes that would prove to be less harmful than trying to abide by anxious assumptions, outlived standards, and external rules.

In nightmares, we are often victims of the parts of ourselves we haven't acknowledged or understood or befriended. If this reality feels nightmarish, we haven't yet seen how enslaved we are by our unacknowledged inner selves; by others who are dreaming their lives from an unacknowledged agenda inside; or by the still largely fear-based institutions of education, marriage, work ethic, laws, income taxes, news media, and government.

In a good dream, a lucid dream, there are no rules about what can or should be. In the best dream humanity could dream for itself, we wouldn't need laws to tell us not to steal. We'd have no need to steal. We'd create and experience plenty for everyone. We wouldn't want to be confined within the walls of imposed lessons that don't apply to our needs, nor would we tolerate our children being compelled to sit at desks silently regurgitating memorized facts onto test papers if what they wanted to be doing was sharing themselves with their friends. We wouldn't have to let things become unbearable before we confronted, learned from, and changed them; and we wouldn't have to blame others for the changes we wanted to make.

But even if this reality is a bad dream, that doesn't mean it isn't valuable. It's our way of communicating with the dreamer behind the dreamers, of getting our unacknowledged selves heeded and responded to, of helping the universe become more consciously creative toward its own best possible dream.

The nightmares are powerful for insight, but the good dreams are just plain wonderful and energizing. A few mornings ago I dreamed that David and Daniel and I had gone to a remote resort, the last resort on the road, which was run by a friend named Regi (Regiment?). The main point of interest was the exploration of the nearby glaciers and icebergs. But as we watched, the ice and snow began to melt. Grass appeared. The temperature of the water had become tropically warm. *What's happening?* Someone asked. *I guess this is the usual change of season*, I answered. *No*, said someone else, *this has never happened before in the memory of recorded history*. All the dangerously shifting ice and snow, a frozen distortion of what lay beneath, was thawing, and the solid ground, colorful and warm, was emerging into spring.

I woke up not knowing if the dream was a personal message for me and David and Daniel, or an indication of what is happening on a grander scale, but either way, I was energized by its promise. Isn't God, the universe, the Great Spirit, the Great Mother, energized by the promise of our good dreams, too? Isn't it worth being a lucid dreamer—living a life of abundance, joy, love, fulfillment, creativity, and freedom—not just for ourselves, but to expand and refresh the One Who is dreaming us?

24

The Physics of Joy

We just finished watching an informative video called *Walking between the Worlds*, in which Gregg Braden demonstrated the physics of joy.

Enthralled by a visually stunning close-up, we sat on the edge of our seats, observing the effect of increasing the frequency of vibrations applied to a drop of water. The pattern created by the frequencies started out as a simple set of concentric rings. It then developed, as the frequencies were raised in quantum leaps of even numbers, into an intricately delicate and exquisite pattern. Having been a six-pointed star and an eight-petaled flower, it became at last a shimmering, overlapping twelve-pointed starflower, awesome to behold. Braden suggested that as we increase our own frequencies—as we consciously intend or allow ourselves to experience more and more of the higher emotional frequencies of joy, happiness, bliss, ecstasy, and divine love—every liquid-filled cell in our bodies resonates into a pattern that connects to and sets off more of the encoded DNA potential than was available to us in lower emotional frequencies. In other words, joy physically enables us, within our very cells, to use much more of what we are capable of being.

To extrapolate: The joy we experience also resonates with anything else outside of ourselves that is of a similarly high frequency and thereby aligns us with it. The happier you are, not just because something external makes you happy, but because you make a conscious decision to feel happy, the more you evolve into being able to use that untapped wellspring of mastery and creativity, and the more you draw to yourself whatever makes your life as wonderful as you want it to be.

It's the best reversal of a Catch 22 I've ever come across—you can't lose.

Something on the outside can make you happy, and your cells will connect with and release even more of your DNA potential, but if nothing on the outside is all that great, you can still use whatever works for you—remembrance of a better past time, hope for a better future time, gratitude, meditation, inspiring music, smelling the roses, going for a run—and by doing so, make sense of the biblical promise, *For he that hath, to him shall be given.*

It's almost a built-in guarantee that humanity, as it blunders through its trials and errors and finally discovers its own capacity for well-being, can and will increase the reality of well-being for the whole planet. Braden proposes that it is the present middle-aged generation that is transforming ages of fear-based duality into an era of loving oneness through its ability to access all of the DNA code with higher emotional frequencies. I propose that it is the generations who are now giving birth and being born who will maintain the high frequencies of worldwide connectedness and consciousness.

The happiness with which you encounter and embrace

everything around you not only amplifies your own sense of well being, it contributes to the evolution of humans into beings of joy and love and masterfully beautiful creations.

Take heed what ye hear: with what measure ye mete, it shall be measured to you; and unto you that hear shall more be given.

25

No Fear

One of the tools of a fear-based society is statistics.

Take, for instance, the number of automobile-related deaths. I don't know what the number is today, but a few years ago I came across the following figures: There was one accident-caused death in the United States every eleven minutes. There were 46,000 deaths in that one year. Thinking that an accident is happening out there somewhere every eleven minutes is going to tend to make you nervous when you get into your vehicle. You're going to strap your kids into the back seat of the most accident-resistant car on the market, the one equipped with airbags and automatic seatbelts and a voice that says buckle up, because that statistic scares you, right? That same statistic, however, translated into another set of figures, adds up to one auto-related death every thirty-seven million vehicle miles. Wow.

Suddenly I'm picturing all those drivers, in all those cities, on all those interstates, in all fifty states, driving all those millions of miles, before one person dies, and I'm thinking, that looks like a whole lot of good driving going on. We *could* be patting ourselves on the back for the incredibly small number of fatal accidents that occurs for the amount of driving we do. I'm not trying to belittle the efforts to make improvements. It is a significant sign of the times that this society is relentlessly striving for perfection in so many areas. I'm just pointing out that the level of national fear concerning driving isn't warranted, and it isn't balanced by the media—not yet, anyway—by giving credit where credit's due.

Another statistic is the number of people dying of starvation. It's horrendous to think that 24,000 people, most of them children, die from malnutrition every day. That adds up to about eight million unnecessary deaths a year. There's no reason for this to be happening. There is more than enough for all of us, and I am very glad that there are people who are doing something about it. In fact, any one of us can do something about it. But lest anyone fear that humanity is an unconscionable species, creating a hell on Earth with its greed and callousness, let's take another look.

Eight million is 0.135% (about 1/8 of one percent) of the world's population. Eight hundred million, which is about how many people are suffering from malnutrition right now, is one out of every 750 people. It's not perfection yet, but twenty years ago, when the world population was smaller, the number of deaths from starvation per year was fourteen million. If I were grading humanity on how well it's doing keeping itself fed, I would have to give it a B+ and cheer it on.

War, to date, has been responsible for the loss of an estimated seventy million lives. Over a hundred thousand deaths are still being caused by wars every year. That means that in all the wars of recorded history, the deaths add up to about 1.5%

of today's world population. About 0.002% of the world's population dies every year in wars. Let's not minimize how atrocious wars are, but let's not lose our perspective here either. How much of the world is at peace?

Let's estimate that besides those who die, the wounded and those left homeless and devastated add up to much more than 0.002%; let's say they add up to a thousand times that much, to 2%. That would still leave 98% of the world that's not in a state of war. Are we doing a much better job of living in harmony than we've been led to believe by the focus on what's considered news? Are we afraid that world peace is an impossible dream? World peace exists! With the exception of a few infected areas that are equivalent to a rash of poison ivy on an otherwise healthy body, vast numbers of people are keeping their acts together, wielding not weapons but tools, providing for their families, interacting in creative communities, trading ideas and skills, and more pervasively than ever, spreading love and consciousness.

A fear-based society tells you that you need insurance because something awful might happen to you. It doesn't tell you that insurance is based on a decent premise: If everyone puts something into a common pot, then those few unfortunates who unconsciously choose to meet with disaster will be provided for. Wouldn't you prefer to know that, based on statistics, your insurance payments are, what, hundreds, thousands of times more likely to be helping out someone else?

A fear-based society uses one mishap to justify the enactment of a law that assumes that everyone else is so clueless they won't be able to prevent the same kind of mishap in their own lives without being threatened with punishment. Wouldn't you like to be able to explain to that police officer that even though you were wearing headphones, you could still hear the radio blasting from the car next to you, but since he's doing such a great job watching out for everybody, you'd be happy to contribute to his pay?

The more we step back and take a look at how subtly fear

pervades human societies, the more we will be able to disem-power its hold on us and realize that we don't even have to work all that hard to re-create our reality. It's already way up there on the scale of deserving congratulations.

26

Role Reversal

David and his friend Dan and I were sitting on the patio after dinner, enjoying the fireflies, the coolness of the evening, and an interesting conversation over a bottle of wine.

A messenger from God interrupted us.

At least, that's how I've concluded I have to regard the visit from a young man who had, years ago, harassed one of the members of my family so obsessively that he had ended up having a restraining order taken out against him. I hadn't seen Trent (not his real name) for years. There had been a time when I had tried to make him feel welcome, had listened to his fearful, angry, funny, twisted ramblings for hours at a time. I had hoped that in time he'd be free of the tormenting delusions that compelled him to make impossibly false accusations about other people. Eventually I began to dread his visits. Those long hours, which I would gladly have shared with any other young person who appeared to be benefiting from expressing his or her emotions, lead nowhere. I could never think of a way to bring them to a closure that was satisfying to both of us.

Finally, one day when more hours of fruitless repetition began unfolding before us, Trent having told me once again that Mozart was visiting him from the Other Side and teaching him how to write music, and having agonized yet again that he might as well kill himself, I thought I'd try a different tactic.

"Why don't you, Trent?" I asked him. "If it's so hard for you on this side, why don't you just kill yourself, and do what Mozart does, teach others to write music from the Other Side?" I thought he might as well explore the option. I even thought it might help him to discover that he didn't really want that option after all. I certainly didn't think I'd get the reaction I got.

"Well!" he exclaimed, getting up. "I can see where I'm not wanted!" And with that, he left.

I was in shock.

You mean all those years . . . it could have been that easy? *The truth will set you free* took on a new meaning for me. He seldom visited me again. That was years ago. In the meantime, he'd been in and out of college, mental institutions, and jail. The last I'd heard, he was living with his brother. The member of my family who had had a restraining order taken out against him had included my address in the off-limits territory, so I expected never to see him again.

David and Dan and I, sitting on the patio, had been discussing a wide variety of interesting topics. We'd also spent some time exploring how we could help create a better situation for Angel, who was, despite Dan's efforts to keep her company during the day, still suffering from imagined governmental surveillance and visits from nonexistent intruders, despite locked doors, when she was alone in David's apartment. Even though she was continuing to say she was moving on, each week to a different town or state, or to a different relative or friend, it wasn't happening. David believed her family didn't care to get involved. We all agreed we wanted to protect her from being forcefully ousted and ending up in a mental institution, but we were at a loss for options.

A car stopped in the driveway, and I couldn't see who was getting out of it until he'd come into the circle of light cast by the patio lamp.

"Hi, Lesta. Who else is here?" Trent peered at the two men beside me.

My reaction was uncalculated and instantaneous. "Trent, you are not welcome here. Please leave." I recoiled from memories of the gun he had carried, the fear he had instilled, the eighty-nine threats recorded on the answering machine that had taken such a toll on someone I cared about.

"I just wanted to . . . "

"I just want you to leave."

"Oh, Christ, I just want to be peaceable . . . "

"I just want you to leave!"

"Oh, well, I can see I'm going to have to pay a visit to the Senator . . . " his voice trailed off as he turned and strode back to his car.

Pleasantly surprised at the ease with which I had just avoided what could have turned messy, I patted myself on the back. But then I noticed what I had just done. In front of David, who is always kind, who constantly keeps in mind that we are all Light Beings, who believes we should all remember to love one another and give one another every chance to heal, in front of this truly good-hearted man, I had just thoughtlessly dismissed another human being. I hadn't even given him a chance to explain his reason for appearing.

And then I remembered my gifts. An impeccably sensitive aura. A self-evident purpose. Trust myself, trust everything I do, I had been reminding myself.

Dan had no problem with the way I'd handled the encounter.

David said gently that maybe the young man had come to make peace.

I defended my behavior, but I wasn't satisfied with the discrepancy between my action and my desire to see David's point of view.

Meanwhile, after Dan left, David began considering whether he should once again assume the role of caretaker and protector for Angel. I was mildly appalled. I'd begun to see an easing of the stress due in part to his having had to constantly shield himself from her negativity and paranoia, and I was eager for him to be able to relax even more.

I remembered something from *The Celestine Prophecy*. "David," I asked him, "as you stand at this fork in the road and look into each direction, which one lights up for you? If you go that way and you see yourself helping one person, and you go that way and you see yourself recovering your ability to help many people, which one draws you?"

"Whichever one I'm shown. It doesn't matter if I have to sacrifice a few months or years of my life, not if that time helps someone heal."

"But your sacrifice will cancel itself out if it drains you the way it did before," I offered lamely, seeing that I wasn't going to be making up his mind for him, no matter how much sense I was making to myself.

There was something about the timing of that visit, I thought as I fell asleep, something I need to know. . . .

I woke up knowing what it was.

If by assuming that the Light is already here, I am participating in its being here, then I do want to assume that it is here, that the world is already enlightened. If the world is already just as it needs to be right now, then Trent and Angel are souls who are serving their purpose just as surely as anyone else is. They are doing what they're meant to do. They are messengers of God as much as anyone is. They are to be respected for their part in David's growth and mine. They are healing us. They are acting as they do to get us to react as we do.

I react by saying go away, somebody else please take over, I don't want to deal with this. That's what comes out. That's what I need to do.

David reacts by wondering if he can help, by going with the flow, by letting things take whatever course demonstrates itself. That's what comes out. That's what he needs to do.

I used to make life so complicated for myself. It's so self-evident. Whatever is, is whatever it is. Tao, baby.

27

Once and Future Past

Until I stood on the steps of the Philadelphia Museum of Art, I'd assumed that other times were tapped into with the mind or with the ethereal essence of oneself. I didn't know we could take our bodies with us, or enter into the bodies we've occupied at other times.

My mother and I, sitting together in my living room, discussed the likelihood of our having been sisters in a past life.

"In Austria?" I was prompted to ask her, seeing in my mind the two of us as young women in a field, at the edge of which stood a colorfully painted oxcart.

"Yes!" she said. "In Austria, I think that's right. When they had those oxcarts with the big wooden wheels, and they painted them with so many bright colors."

"Oh my gosh, that's what I just saw, too," I told her.

"We lived on a farm!" she said.

"Yes, I see a field that's been mown, some kind of golden grain gathered into bunches." I tried to hone in on a date. 1673 came to mind.

"I think it was in the 1600s," my mother said before I'd opened my mouth.

"Yes! In the 1670s, yes!"

"But you left me. I didn't know what happened to you," my mother said wistfully, taking my hand. "I'm so glad you're with me now."

A scene flashed through my mind as I squeezed her hand. I had left my younger sister at the farmhouse, and I was out beyond the field, on my way into the woods, when a soldier grabbed me. A chill shivered through my body at the memory. He had raped me, and then, frightened by the possible consequences of what he had done, he had jammed his bayonet into my abdomen and killed me.

I told my mother what I'd just seen.

"Oh, my sweetie, I never knew. No wonder I was so happy to have you back with me when you were born!" She had told me often that my arrival was one of the most treasured events of her life.

"Did they have bayonets in Austria in the 1600s?" I asked. Neither of us knew. I pulled out a volume of the encyclopedia and looked it up. The bayonet had become a weapon of war in Europe in the mid-1600s. The uniform of the soldiers was exactly as I had seen it. I remembered more. And the more I remembered, the more I was certain that I knew who the soldier was in this lifetime, and why we had met again.

But that was a memory, scenes flashing into our minds as my mother and I sat in the comfort of my living room, putting the past behind us and delighting in our reunion all over again.

As I stood at the top of the steps of the Philadelphia Museum of Art, overlooking the fountains and the traffic circles lined with trees, the city scene before me began to waver as if dissolved by heat waves, and I found myself standing on a grassy knoll on the riverbank, overlooking a wild marshy meadow, having just wandered here from upriver. Suddenly, I was startled by a transparent vision of the future that made no sense. It was so imposing and alien, towering hardness with shimmering water surfaces, rounded forms of gleaming colors moving below, enormous carvings of humans and animals. The vision faded and the meadow returned to normal, but I stood there momentarily stunned by what I'd seen. I didn't look down at myself to see who I was. I was me, in my scanty animal-skin coverings, alone on the riverbank, with no interfering thoughts racing through my mind, for my language was simple and didn't demand to be heard or framed into stories. I wouldn't be telling anyone what I'd seen.

But for a moment I'd known something, and it made my world both more intimate and vaster. I saw that this marshy meadow was not permanent. I looked into its depths and saw that it had accumulated over time, that it had undulated through time, that it had once been much lower, and steaming, but there was something physically dangerous about then, so I withdrew. The vision of the future was not dangerous so much as overpoweringly complex, and yet it made me sad, but then I knew that there was a future beyond that one, in which there was no trace of what had been.

I snapped back to the sounds of traffic and people talking around me and found myself in the future of a long-forgotten past, gazing down at the Franklin Parkway.

From Rock with Wings, years later, I took a day trip to the pueblo ruins of Chaco Canyon and was walking among the flat-stone structures when I found myself listening to the children laughing. They ran past me, naked and brown and supple, toward where several of the women of my tribe were chopping squash, preparing a meal. Suddenly I grew enormously sad, for even though I was dressed in leather and my skin was brown from the sun, I sensed that someday I would return here in strange thin clothing with pale skin, and I would look at my village in ruins. I saw what I would see then, that my people had long since disappeared.

I shook off the vision of the future and wandered from building to building with enhanced affection for what would not last. I thought of my time in the circular birthing room, and how the father of our children had sat with our brothers in the other circular room, seeking visions for the names of their newborns. I followed the path to the farther cluster of buildings, where he had lived before we built our own room, industriously laying flat rock upon flat rock, day after day, until we were sheltered from the sun. I loved that our children had added their own sleeping rooms to our living quarters when they were old enough to want their privacy. I passed the kiva, silently enjoying my memories of its double use, for sacred ceremonies and for entertainment—drama and storytelling—on long winter evenings. I went to the river, and again the future imposed itself on me. One day it would be nothing but a dry channel, and my people's children's children would have to move on.

Again some younger, pale woman who would someday be me, returning to this home of mine, tugged at me. Ah, but I was old enough to let her pull some wisdom from me. I released my reluctance and poured what I knew toward her, so that when she came back, she would remember this feeling of community and family, the beauty of this way of life.

When I came to, surrounded by the remains of an ancient village being examined by tourists with cameras and brochures in their hands, everything looked transparent.

I returned to Rock with Wings that evening, knowing as I approached that I would have to visit the cave again the next morning, where I'd left my diamond-shaped stone. I parked in the desert beside the double-tracked trail, about a fifteen-minute walk from the Rock, and slept in my van with the side door open, beneath the brilliant stars. The next morning, as I pulled on my hiking boots and filled my goatskin canteen with water, a red four-wheel-drive vehicle drove past my parked van toward the ridge near the base of the Rock. Even though we were the only two visitors to this vast stretch of sacred land, the blond driver ignored me. He parked, got out of his vehicle, a camera slung over his shoulder, and climbed to the ridge. Instead of taking a picture, he faced the stone ridge, leaned his arm against it, and leaned his head against his arm. Feeling intrusive watching him take this position of apparent despondency, I turned and headed up the base toward the cave, soon out of sight of this person who obviously needed to be alone.

Perhaps an hour later, elated with the discovery of my initial in a diamond formed of twigs and my little stone turned star-side up, feeling opened again to hope and faith and eagerness, I headed back down the slope, leaping from boulder to boulder. The red vehicle was no longer in sight. I trekked across the desert floor toward my distant van, when suddenly a wave of nauseous anxiety overcame me. I moaned and almost doubled over, stumbling across a pair of fresh tire tracks, wondering what was happening to me, but within a few steps I felt fine again. I frowned, shrugged, and walked on, starting to think about the crackers and tuna fish in my cooler, and was only a few yards from my van when I was hit again by an overwhelming wave of fear and hopelessness. Groaning, I stumbled forward, but this time, noticing how quickly I recovered, I looked back, and saw the cause. I had just crossed the fresh tire tracks again.

In this remote place of purity and power, the energy left by the driver of the red vehicle was unmistakably intact. I wondered how people could survive in a city, where trails of energy crisscross every inch of walking space. What I'd experienced in Chaco Canyon, in contrast, had not been a tapping into energies left there long ago. It had been mine.

Now I know why I tend to compare what's happening in our society not only with an ideal that comes from a future of blissful harmony, but also with an innate standard of tribal values, devoid of superimposed, distantly contrived laws and governed only by the immediate needs of the people involved.

How fortunate I am that an ancient woman, living intimately with the land, in love with its beauty and with the beauty of her people, poured herself into me when I most needed to remember and recover my soul.

Or did I pour myself into her? Are there any boundaries, really? No. All time is now. Now I'm beginning to understand that gift of memory of past and future.

When my three-year-old daughter and I drove past her cousin's house instead of stopping there as we had every other time, she turned around in her seat, craning to keep an eye on it, and asked in amazement, "Where's Kyndi's house going?"

I can walk from one end of a railroad car to another, watching the landscape fly by, and adjust my perception to accommodate more than what my eyes are telling me. It isn't the landscape that's flying by blurringly fast nearby and comparatively slow way out there; it's me in my little time capsule that's moving past an unmoving countryside; and it isn't those mountains that are so tiny I can fit them into the circle of my thumb and forefinger; it's me that is dwarfed by their immensity.

As my perception gradually becomes inclusive enough to see the whole tree instead of just my leaf, I begin to understand that the gift of memory is the same gift as lucid dreaming. As paradox. As astral travel. As all of them.

I'd forgotten, so I could enjoy the indescribable pleasure of rediscovering, my infinite and eternal experience.

I'd forgotten, so I could enjoy the indescribable pleasure of my tiny, insignificant little life's tiny, insignificant little moments. "Eric," I asked my three-year-old son, "don't you want to put on a shirt? It's getting cool outside." He pulls on an adult-sized T-shirt and flies out the door yelling, "Here I come! I'm Supermarket!"

28

Warned and Welcome

I've had two warning dreams. The first one was in the format of a movie.

Scene: a man visible from the knees down, with just his trousers and shoes showing, is passing a phone booth. He hears a tiny pleading voice and pauses. In the corner of the phone booth is crumpled a broken, talking, puppet-like doll, appealing to him to pick it up.

Scene: a man has brought home a brand-new talking puppet-like doll for his sweetheart, who finds it intriguing and clever. She puts it on the mantelpiece and hugs him.

Scene: the man and his girlfriend have started arguing. The argument escalates into shouts. She lashes out at him, scratching his face, drawing blood, and he swings back. Suddenly a flood of churning water and debris that comes crashing through their house tears them from one another.

Scene: the man, his face scratched and his clothes damp, has wandered into a roomful of people who are all swearing off ever picking up talking icons again. They are reinforcing one another's resolve, like recovering addicts, having discovered that merely having the broken puppets in their possession ruins their lives. They need constant support to resist the pleas, because the icons are everywhere.

Scene: a man visible from the knees down, with just his trousers and shoes showing, has paused beside a phone booth. A broken doll is wheedling at him coyly from the corner of the phone booth. The trousers and shoes move on, leaving the puppet behind. What looks like credits scrolls over the scene, but the words say at the end: "This has been an important message."

In the second dream, I'm in what feels like a halfway house. People are going around in circles, doing the same things over and over again. I'm backing away, easing myself along the wall toward the door, hoping I won't be noticed.

In the next scene, I'm in the forest, following a trail beneath the beautiful tall trees, when I remember that I've left something back at the house, which is perhaps a quarter of a mile behind me. I pause, wondering if I should go back for it. I turn around, not even sure of what it is I didn't want to leave behind, but before I can take a step, I see a figure in a white linen robe and sandals approaching me. It's Jesus. He has brought me what I'd forgotten to take, a glass in which is still about an inch of golden-tea-colored liquid, the last of what I'd almost finished drinking before I left. He hands it to me and with a gesture indicates that I should finish it. I drink the clear golden liquid, and thank him silently for having stopped me from returning to the house of useless repetition, and then, understanding why he has appeared, I turn into my new direction to find where I belong, somewhere beautiful and wholesome and uplifting and inspiring.

As a youngster, I could not justify my having more than

others—more creative parents, more land to roam, more under the Christmas tree, more talent, more laughter with my siblings. So I didn't keep things. I gave them away. Finally I almost gave away my life, because I couldn't see how I deserved to have so much. Perhaps this whole book so far has been a series of justifications. Perhaps I am trying to tell *myself* more than anyone that it's okay to *have*: happiness, gifts, support, freedom from guilt, freedom from feeling responsible for everyone in the world. I try to remember that each person has his or her own destiny, and it's okay, it's better than okay, for me not to interfere. I've come to where I'm telling myself maybe I'm not really all that spiritual after all, because I really don't *care* what happens to some people. I don't care so much that I could just possibly become a banshee on wheels if they interfere with anyone I do care about.

Someone is expecting David to put his gifts on hold in order to maintain her sense of safety. If it were just about me, I would say go, man, go, do whatever you need to do, and I'll do whatever I need to do, alone. I'll be fine. I'd rather see you use your gifts in this way than in that, but that's not for me to decide. But David has already decided how he wants to use his gifts. That's why he's here instead of there. He's trying to ignore the talking broken puppet. He's trying to leave the house of repetition, too, just like me. But Angel is outraged; she's accusing him of not communicating with her about what's going on, or, more to the point, about whether he's going to return to his role of protector.

How do we define the fine lines between compassion, enlightenment, and indifference?

Help me out here, somebody. Where's that whisper off to the left somewhere? Anybody? Please? Off to the right? Over my head?

Okay, woman, calm down.

Oh, you *are* here! I've been missing you!

You've been missing having to divide yourself to see the problem from the outside?

121

No, I've been missing seeing the problem from the outside. What's it look like from out there? I just can't seem to turn it around from in here.

It looks like you're doing a whole lot of detrimental worrying.

Detrimental? Useless, I can understand. Unnecessary. But detrimental? What do you mean?

Let me try to explain something to you. What you project is what your environment will become.

You mean, like, if you interpret a friendly situation as hostile because you still regard everyone in terms of a past experience that infused you with paranoia, then that situation does feel hostile?

No. We are not talking about a filter through which your perception of reality is colored. We are talking about the observer actually changing the observed. We are talking about how the universal energy that is brought into focus by you superimposes an image, as if passing through a slide in a projector, onto your environment, an image, which is then actually materialized, because it is through you that reality is created.

Hmm. Tell me more.

Whatever happens to you and around you is what you, as a creatively focusing instrument, have projected. If you, as a channel for universal energy, are encumbered with cloudy emotions—for instance, the fear that things will not turn out for the best—then what gets projected includes the images conjured up by this cloudy emotion, and you find yourself indeed in a situation in which things are not turning out for the best.

You mean, certain emotions smudge the slide in the projector?

They create images on the slide. As do clear emotions. If your instrument, your channel, your mind, your projector, is filled with, for instance, the loving confidence that the best that can happen is happening, if the slide through which you project the universal energy is a clear picture of what you really want, let's say, for instance, comfort and financial stability, if it has actual images in it of the house you want to live in, the trips you want to take, the people to whom you want to give gifts, the abundant time you need to be of service doing what you love to do, then that projected image superimposes itself on your environment, and your environment shifts itself to materialize the physical reality of the picture. Whatever thoughts and feelings you have, whether they arise in you from an echo of the past or are created by you as the new future you want for yourself, those thoughts and feelings go into the image on the slide, get projected into your surroundings, and materialize.

An echo of the past. As in repetition. As in my dream.

Yes. The icon, the broken puppet in your dream, represents the once-damaged self—in anyone—that can only repeat the thoughts and feelings of helplessness, victimization, desperate survival by cunning manipulation. An addiction to these repetitions continues to project them into reality. When you leave these repetitions behind and drink the Christ Consciousness into yourself, you cleanse the projector, you clear out the channel, you put in a new slide, a clean slate, as it were, and you are free to imagine—to create an image of—whatever will bring you joy, love, harmony, wisdom, generosity of spirit. That image will materialize itself into being, into a reality at least as wonderful as what you projected, if not better. Do you understand?

Oh, my, I hope I understand! I hope I can remember this!

Then hope is what your environment will reflect to you.

Oh. Yes. I see. Thank you. I am confident that the best that *can* happen *is* happening.

So be it.

29

Over the Sill

The mimosa tree is attracting butterflies. Above the feathery puffs of pink and white and the delicate fern-patterned leaves, silently floating on wings of yellow, brown, and orange, flutter these peaceful little beings of myth and transformation. Even as the grass beneath the tree dries into a blanched mat of thin straw, for we are suffering the worst drought in seventy years, the butterflies avail themselves of sweetly fragrant nectar. While the farmers in our area are harvesting one rolled bale of alfalfa instead of six and wondering how they'll feed their dairy cows come winter, the butterflies are prospering. When their time comes, they will fade, but they will have given their colors to anyone who wants a respite from intensity and density and gravity. As I watch them, I can almost feel that thirteenth door opening, the one through which I can step once I've mastered all the gifts.

Does that mean that all paradoxes fit into my reality? That I finally see everything that happens as the guidance I need? Am I acting as the unique culmination and source of all the influences coming into and out of me? Do I see everyone and everything as a reflection of the One? Have I learned to gentle my experiences with peace? Do I trust the intelligence of my aura? Has my purpose become, from moment to moment, self-evident? Have I mastered astral travel as a means of accomplishing what I need to when nothing else serves as well? Do I remember that all time is now? Do I know I'm dreaming, and therefore I can dream my dream as I intend to? Am I waking up happy every morning, grateful for everything in my life? Am I indeed ageless?

Well . . . maybe I'm not over the sill yet. But something's telling me I'm getting there.

Hot flashes.

When I first started having them, they were a gentle surprise, similar to the secret I harbored when I was pregnant, when that somebody developing inside me first began to stir. No one else was aware in the same intimate way of the relationship that was forming between me and whoever was going to emerge. I refused to take any drugs that would have minimized experiencing the stages of my pregnancy. I might have endangered, or at the least numbed, two lives' peak experiences. I didn't even want any medication when the emergence of another being from inside me became so imminent that I began to experience more bone-wrenching, hip-stretching pain than I'd ever believed my body capable of enduring. Nothing in my life has been as profoundly memorable as the culmination of that excruciating pain—feeling like I was being literally, laterally ripped open and turned inside out—suddenly giving way to the most exquisitely wondrous, absolutely pain-free and awesome elixir of holding in my arms the little being I'd been nurturing into the world.

So *of course* I'm not going to take anything to deactivate these new sensations of transformation. *Some* of us have to champion the natural way, right?

Still pregnant with my emerging self, I am soon introduced to the less seductively intimate face of a hot flash—the much more public flush of a debilitating three-minute fever, sizzling away all the stuff my body, mind, and soul don't have any more use for. I endure these mini volcanic eruptions with the same teeth-gritting gratitude I have for my body's wisdom when it has put me on hold during the flu, running at emergency efficiency to return me to health. *Okay*, I take a deep breath after another labor pain. *I can do this.*

I start waking up kicking off the covers with menace on my mind and diving for the window to gulp in cool air. I'm burning with energy in the middle of the freaking night, I grumble to myself, turning on the light at 3:00 A.M. and sweating for action. I'm prevented from starting up the vacuum cleaner by a mighty thin thread of consideration for people who are sleeping in their way cool bodies that don't have hot flashes.

The hot flashes become alarming. Something isn't *right* here. I'm stewing like a pot of over-seasoned chili that would make flames come out of your eyes. I'm so hot under the collar I could throw the Samsonite gorilla right through the bars of his cage. Roarrrr!! But if Joan of Arc could burn for her passionate truth . . .

This new self is so raw. It feels everything directly. It isn't like the hardened encasement I've wrapped myself up in to be able to carry out my duties for so many years. It has intuitions that are vivid and insistent, and if I refuse to acknowledge them . . . well, maybe I'm not supposed to refuse to acknowledge them.

This brilliant deduction leads to a brilliant discovery.

On those days that I give my new self true freedom, I don't have hot flashes!

A few days ago I arranged to have no one to answer to by any certain time, and I found a stream, and I waded into it and collected rocks. For hours, I was a child discovering treasures to my heart's content, with no one around to tell me it was time to go home or to do something else. I found rocks that told me they wouldn't mind becoming part of a work of art that would get people to look at rocks differently, to look at them and see that they are alive and well in *los mundos*. I brought them home with me and arranged them into a sculptural gathering of rocks. They didn't mind being glued together; it happens to them in nature, under the ground. Why, this was even better, being held in place as visible representatives of the stone people. They knew I loved them, and they showed me where to place them to their best advantage.

I didn't have one hot flash the entire day.

When I started writing this, I was under the impression that women my age would be the only people empathetic enough to appreciate my superhuman stamina. But David says he's had hot flashes, every once in a while, for years. Oh? Yes, and he always thought of them as the result of being supercharged with Light. He knows he leaves his body at night, and when he returns from the realm of Light, he wakes up in a sweat. He's always thought of the excessive heat as accompanying an expansion of his Light Being self within his material form. Which is basically the conclusion I was just coming to for myself. Like so many women, I've spent years emotionally, biologically, and socially equipped to be a nurturer, sensitive to the needs of others. It wasn't at the expense of myself. It was myself. But there's more of me waiting for its time, and its time is now. That doesn't mean I give up who I was. It means I burst forth with more of who I am becoming.

I tried once to remember my own birth. I succeeded in recapturing a hazy, numbed sense of being in the birth canal. I was in a stupor. I was robbed of one of the most powerful experiences of this life of mine because my mother was drugged.

But when I took myself further back in time, I found my memory of my conception to be intact. What a surprise. I could remember being both the sperm and the egg at the same time. As the egg, I rolled slowly through the immensity of an undulating tunnel, a universe unto myself, complete, eternal, yet sensing that I was about to be changed forever. As the sperm, I was one of many life forms urgently racing toward some goal as the agent of change. As the egg, I felt anxious about the upcoming changes: were they mine to determine? Would I lose what I had been? As the sperm, I was supremely confident that I was the one. I was the chosen representative of all the others, no matter how quickly I projected myself forward, or how slowly, I would get there, the way would be prepared for me, and the change I would initiate would be incredible, stupendous.

As the egg, I felt accosted. So many attempts to penetrate my vastness, and then suddenly I am unalterably imploded-exploded from my eternal singularity into dimension, size, division, and multiplication. I am growing smaller and greater; I am reducing and expanding; I am funneled into form, bringing the memory of my Oneness with me. As the sperm, I am rejoicing; I have reached my goal; I have changed everything; I have merged with immensity and part of me is given into every new version of what I am becoming.

Letting that memory surface brought into focus a theme or family trait given to me by each of my parents. My mother, although she loved people and parties, was deep down inside, self-protective, anxious about being forced to deal with reality, and forever longing to reconnect with Spirit. My father, who tended to keep to himself much of the time, was unassailably confident of his role in life, and confident of his success and power in this world.

This memory had been triggered by a preceding event. Several years ago, I was invited to the house of an acquaintance to watch a video on channeling. The living room was packed with eagerly interested people. After the viewing of the film, we all gathered around a table of refreshments. A petite, frail Afro-American woman with short-bobbed gray hair and a flower-print cotton dress hanging from her thin shoulders looked up at me and touched my arm. I looked down at her, and my heart began to melt and flood. Wordlessly, she took my large pale hand into her small bony dark ones and held it within the dry warmth of her grasp. Tears of recognition filled my eyes, and hers. She patted my arm, my cheek, and then we embraced, holding on to one another, so glad to be holding on to one another again at last, for a long, long, gently swaying moment.

I wanted to call her grandmother in a language I didn't know, but I'd never seen Lavinia before in my life.

I ached for her when I left. I tried to remember from when I'd known her. . . .

I was a little brown-skinned girl, sitting on the dusty ground, leaning my arms on her knee. Her deep-set eyes sparkled at me as she patted my small dark hand. Around us, tall brown women in turbans and draped garments squeezed and unfurled and snapped and spread out large rectangles of colorful fabrics—saffron, rusty orange, and tangerine—to dry on the bank of a lazy butterscotch river lined with graceful trees. They were smiling and glancing at one another, because each of them had sat at Mamau's knee as I was doing now, being reminded of their beginnings.

"Oh, yes, I can remember all the way back to when there were two of me," she was saying, and I, too, could remember when there were two of me. I could remember being a vast, timeless sphere of solitude, being approached by change, and oh how excited I was for the change, how I welcomed it, how I would embrace what would change me. And I could remember being life-sized, for life was all around me for comparison, racing toward . . . what? Toward what impossible goal? What a hopeless ambition to try to reach this goal with so many others competing. As the great sphere, I opened with love to receive all these tiny flutterings around me. And as the small life form, I was surprised and humbled and grateful, for it was I who entered, I who had been chosen to experience this astounding explosion into ecstasy, into infinitely, astonishingly wonderful expansion.

"Oh, yes," Mamau said, seeing in my eyes what I was seeing. "There are those whose two-of-me's were not so harmonious in their union. Their two ways of being in the world are in conflict with one another. But you were conceived in love. Yes. So now you understand."

I understood how my mother's warm and ample love for my hesitant, uncertain father had transformed him into the gentle and peaceful man he was. I understood the singular gifts that had been passed into me from each of their lineages. I reached up and threw my arms around Mamau, and was held tightly in a warm embrace that would last through transformations, a memory so enduring it would bring tears of recognition to my eyes when I saw Mamau as Lavinia for a single, brief moment in this lifetime.

How I treasure what she taught me.

We can be the proud owners of all the nuances and complexities of our transitions.

How sad that so many people fear their own breakthroughs, or for the sake of society's convenience find it necessary to mute their changes with drugs. How sad that they must shortchange themselves of their fullest experiences so that they will fit into the machine, when honoring the changes in themselves could trigger such needed changes in the system. But the time will come—we will know—when we can re-create ourselves as effortlessly as we can fulfill our dreams.

When I was pregnant with my daughter, her father and I went for counseling. He wanted to get married and I didn't. I did want him to be our child's actively involved father. I just didn't want to be his actively involved wife. (As it turned out, he's been a wonderful father. I would have been a disappointing wife.) I prefaced our first session with a disclaimer. "If I turn red," I said, "I just want you to know that it isn't because I'm embarrassed or angry. I tend to have these heat waves flush through me because I'm pregnant." I look back and shake my head at having disowned the wisdom of my body in transition. When I flush red, I *am* embarrassed or angry. When I'm having a hot flash, I'm embarrassed by my lack of confidence, fearful of falling back into answering to others, angry for not being true to the real me, roaring at how much I need to break out of my past. Those who follow will have so much less to break out of, but in the meantime, my own cocoon is splitting, and I'm noticing it. What a great alarm system, what necessary labor pains, what a harbinger of major changes are these rises in the temperature of my bloodstream. *Am* I going to douse them, regulate them, normalize them? What, and squelch the being inside me who wants to come out strong and clear and balanced and whole? Not on my life. This transition is mine, all mine. It's my secret relationship, my burning fever of healing, my shedding of too tight a compartment, my emergence into someone nine feet tall and shining, thank you very much.

I'm not over the sill yet, but I don't mind standing in the doorway, being stripped naked, no matter how much it scares me. I'm freeing my butterfly wings.

30

Like a Duck to Water

Every time I get out of my car, Hewlett and Packard waddle over, quacking noisily, and dip their heads up and down in greeting.

At least I think it's in greeting.

Maybe it's because they're hungry. Maybe they just don't want me petting the cats. Maybe they're trying to tell me something. They get really insistent sometimes.

Hewlett gets to where he (oh, yes, he has two curled tail feathers now—what can I say?) is no longer nibbling; he is taking hold of my flesh and trying to rip it off. I watch the skin on my arm get stretched out into a peak before it snaps back, bruised red, and I think to myself, this duck is trying to tell me something.

Packard, meanwhile, is diving at me with unclear intentions, practically crawling into my lap and then flapping back-
wards and standing there quacking, his velvety green head
going up and down, and he will not be dismissed. He follows
me by walking right in front of my feet, outguessing my every
step, keeping my pace accompanied with a constant low-voiced
wah-wah-wah. So I am getting out of the car, being assaulted,
being forced to watch my step to avoid the juicy splatters on
the brick path, and I scan the yard, which looks like someone
just had a major pillow fight, downy feathers scattered everywhere, and I make a decision.

My daughter and Daniel and I park the van by the local
public lake, open the side door, open the large carton in the
back, and coax our quiet, watchful duckies onto the dry grass
and toward the water.

We are greeted by a flock of not very wild Canadian geese
on the lookout for handouts, and our duckies huddle close to
one another as they hurry to keep up with us. A few mallards,
dwarfed by Packard's healthy glow, speak duckese to them, and
they answer, not quite sure what to make of this community.
Even the expanse of the lake is more intimidating than it is
inviting. My heart sinks, but my daughter encourages me to
encourage the duckies into the water. They test it hesitantly,
and after a brief wetting, climb ashore over the low rocks and
let us know they're ready to go home now.

Again we lead them to the water, one of us feeding the
geese to keep them engrossed at a distance while the other
splashes the water with her hand. The duckies plop themselves
into the shallows again and start plucking at the algae, and one
of them comes up with what looks like a chicken bone in his
beak. Or a duck bone? Eeyew. Grosser than gross. I don't know
about this. Daniel has a suggestion. Let's take them back home
and try again tomorrow. Sigh. This is not looking good. Especially when we pique the interest of by far the ugliest creature on
the lake. Swimming lopsidedly, its lumpy red head reminiscent
of a turkey buzzard, its pale freckled feet suggesting anemia, its

feathers apparently glued on, one from every other fowl on the lake, it decides to become the official welcoming committee. I'm ready to agree with Daniel and Hewlett and Packard. Let's go home. But Fawni suggests that instead of being overprotective, let's leave them overnight and visit them tomorrow and see how they're doing. I guess she's tired of wiping duck poop off the bottom of her shoes, too.

We leave them a handful of their favorite kibbled cat food and make a dash for the van, looking back with sinking hearts as our vulnerable, super-healthy duckies wander among the dusty-looking geese on shore, wondering where they are, wondering where we are.

On my way to working part time at a frame shop the next day, I stop at the lake. No duckies to be seen. Uh oh . . . ? Oh! There they are, out in the middle of the water, near the island. Wow, they made it through the night. They're looking pretty good from here. They're looking actually radiant, gleaming with robust health, and, look at that, still accompanied by the turkey-buzzard half-breed, flapping their wings and preening their feathers as if they've lived here all their lives.

"Duckies!" After hearing a half dozen of my calls, they finally decide to swim casually toward me, plucking at the water's surface on the way, followed by their ever-faithfully adoring misfit. The sight of my outstretched hand adds a bit of speed to their approach, and they eagerly accept my offering of kibble, but there's no way they're getting out of the water, in case I was wondering. In fact, they really don't have that much time for me. There's just too much swimming to do.

On my return visit at the end of the workday, I once again bring kibble, and this time several graceful, long-necked, wide-eyed Canadian geese are hopeful of a helping. Wrong. Hewlett isn't about to let these ladies horn in on his human's provisions. He clears them away with an aggressive lunge here and there, and when he returns to attack my handful of cat food with jackhammer speed, Packard takes a turn at keeping the geese at bay. He goes so far as to climb aboard one of them as she flaps away, pawing the water with her wings to get out from under him.

Satisfied that the free food is gone, these two utterly transformed creatures proudly cut two V's across the water in the direction of the island, followed by their one-leg-is-not-both-the-same fan club, whom, I noticed, they did not chase away from the tossed handfuls of kibble.

"The duckies rule!" I report to Fawni, who has meanwhile also visited them and is as ecstatic as I am at the success of our endeavor.

The next day, my once-stepdaughter Raine and her son Eli and I rent a paddleboat and witness yet another transformation. Hewlett and Packard are an integrated part of the community, swarming around our tossed handfuls of corn with about two dozen geese, mallards, and smaller white ducks until the food has run out, and then grazing lazily in the shallows under the willows. They have taken to their new life like a duck takes to water.

If there are no coincidences—or, as I like to think, if our stories are so masterfully executed by cooperative authors and Author that every event is meaningfully interwoven into the flow of the plot—then I've just been given an insight into the behavior of David's ex-girlfriend, who continues to verbally assault him. Like the ducks, she doesn't know why she's so frustrated. She doesn't know what it is she needs; all she knows is that something's gotta give, and he seems to be the agent of change, so what is he going to do? She belongs somewhere, and someone has to figure out where, and even if it doesn't look all that promising at first, it's very possible that she could end up a whole lot happier than she is right now.

What do ducks know? They know what heaven is supposed to feel like, and they know when they're not in it, and they know when they are.

31

A Good Sign

I'm going to put a new sign up at the yellow gate.

The yellow metal gate was put across the path by Met Ed to protect its power-line right-of-way. Before the gate was installed, the path led right off the tree-lined dirt road toward the field. It curves along the edge of the spruce trees and crosses a clearing into mysterious woods, reminiscent of some medieval Celtic forest, dusky and secretive. The path emerges from the trees into a clearing, and leads to a pond, a placid oval mirror completely surrounded by leafy trees. (If it weren't for several snapping turtles who have made this pond their home, I would have brought Hewlett and Packard here—and they would have missed out on their new life.) Bullfrogs, crickets, and cicadas all chorus their own songs at different times of the day. Occasionally a flock of crows passes overhead, cawing, and sometimes a tall blue heron can be seen in the shaded shallows on the other side. When a breeze shimmers across the surface of the water, it silvers the deep reflection of the clouds.

I used to have to go through these woods carrying a trash bag, which would be half full of beer bottles, empty cigarette packs, toilet paper, condoms, and soda cans by the time I hoisted it into the trash can at the yellow gate.

These days, it seems, things are changing, everywhere. There's very little trace of whatever visitors have come through. I know they've been here. I've heard them making happy sounds at the rope swing on this side of the pond, and a few weeks ago I encountered a young couple taking an afternoon walk.

"Is this your land?" the young woman asked.

"Mine to watch over," I answered. "I don't mind you being here. Please enjoy yourselves. Just don't leave any trash," I requested out of habit.

"Oh, don't worry!" she assured me. "It's much too beautiful here." And then she asked, out of nowhere, "Are you a healer?"

What a lovely sign of the times, her asking that question.

I used to have to frequently replace my please-don't-litter sign. It would get taken, tossed, or smashed.

Now I'm going to put up a new sign:

WELCOME
IF YOU ARE HERE BECAUSE
YOU ARE IN PAIN, COME IN,
FEEL FREE TO TELL IT,
IT WILL BE HEARD.
IF YOU ARE HERE TO FIND SOME PEACE,
COME IN, LET YOURSELF BE GIVEN TO
BY NATURE.
IF YOU ARE HERE TO SHARE
YOUR JOY, AS OTHERS HAVE BEFORE YOU,
YOU TOO ARE AWAITED.

David leans back in his chair and peruses my computer screen. "No, no, no," he says. "What do you mean, 'Welcome'? You want hordes of people coming here? That sign should read: 'If you are in pain, go away! If you're here for some peace, take a piece of your trash with you! Donations are accepted.'" He turns back to his computer and mutters something at it.

"I'm going to put up two signs, one with your words on it, and your name signed to it," I threaten.

"What do you think of this background?" he addresses his enlightened-stories Web page.

I lean against his arm and check out his screen. "I don't like it," I tell him.

He changes it, using a program that creates random patterns, which can be mirrored in several directions. He's getting some very ethereal effects, wispy traces of pale aqua blue against indigo, suggestive of angel wings . . .

"There you go, that's it," I cry out at his seventh attempt.

"What? That orange is too ugly." He saves it.

"Aw done," his computer tells him in a little girl's voice.

"Thank you, dearie," he responds.

"Now I know what I have to say at the end of giving you a massage," I note.

"Thank you, dearie," he says, taking the hint.

Is the forest being appreciated more because there are good feelings spreading outward from this house into the surrounding land, or is the whole world changing? Either way, it looks like a good sign to me.

32

Dear Deer

We parked the van at the one last available campsite in the Canaan Valley State Park, a welcome discovery after an all-night drive to the area where David's family reunion was going to be held. David and Daniel and I got out and stretched, looking over our good fortune—this had to be the loveliest spot in the campground, way at the end of the looped road, surrounded by oaks and maples at the edge of a forest of curly-rooted evergreens.

As we began to unpack our provisions, a doe appeared, about ten feet away. She nibbled delicately at a few heart-shaped leaves as we held our breath in awe. I reached for my camera in slow motion. I needn't have been so cautious. By the time we'd set up our tents and arranged our coolers and stove on the picnic table, she had come even closer, pricking her ears at us curiously. I sat down on a boulder and spoke to her. She flicked her tail, walked right up to me, and touched her nose to my hand. I was enchanted.

By our fourth morning, not only had she accepted carrots from David and let Daniel pet her graceful neck, she had brought her yearling daughter, a creamy-coated, hesitant, feminine creature, and her twin fawns, still speckled and furry, to browse through our homey, open-aired abode. She and two other does, whom we learned to recognize by their slight differences in color and markings, knew only humans who were trustworthy, peaceful, content, and appreciative. We had found a little plot of heaven in the mountains of West Virginia, where humans and animals lived in harmony.

Even the black bear that lumbered across the meadow in front of David's aunt's house was cheered on as he approached the dumpster behind the nearby restaurant. We could see from Aunt Gin's driveway that the dining room windows were crowded with onlookers. When a busboy tried to shoo away the hungry visitor, he was booed by a lawn full of relatives. As the bear pulled a trash bag from the dumpster and loped off with its booty, it was accompanied by a round of applause. Aunt Gin and her daughter Sharon didn't mind having to clean up the trail of inedible garbage on the other side of their garden. In fact, they were delighted to announce the next morning that the bear had brought a friend along on its later forage, and we should just go take a look at the depth of those tracks they left: why, they were three inches deep, but you know, a bear can leave no tracks at all if it doesn't want to. Had we been to the Blackwater River yet to look for fossils?

Yes, we had, and David had found the same rock—with the indentations of two tree branches on it—that he had regretted leaving behind two years ago. The same one, only it turned out to be five times as big as he'd thought it was, once he'd dug it out of the stream. He had lugged it to the van, and we had continued along the twenty-mile wilderness road, which was so narrowly cut between the pines that it would have been impossible to turn around if the river was too high where we'd have to cross it.

There had been a serious downpour the week before, which we figured out only when we came to the results of the flooding. The road was so washed out, Daniel and I had to walk ahead and direct David over the protruding rocks and around the deepest potholes. If he had hit bottom and cracked the oil pan, or worse, we would have had a half-day's walk back to civilization. We'd been warned about the rattlers and copperheads. For several miles we walked, directed, rode on the bumper, trekked ahead again, soaked our shoes testing the depth of the creek and the puddles, and finally emerged, the three of us, muddy, victorious, and exhilarated.

We were in heaven. We were a team. I was meeting wonderful people who had come from three or four different states to share their stories and memories—eighty-year-olds who were raving about their computers and preparing huge amounts of food, and brothers and uncles and cousins who teased and laughed and spent hours walking the river's edge looking for fossils. David had finally fulfilled his promise to his son that he would someday take him camping, and Daniel was thoroughly enjoying it, carving himself a staff to match his father's, gathering firewood with a flashlight, and toasting marshmallows over a dreamy campfire. We were having the best possible vacation.

So the dream I had one morning was puzzling. If it was a dream. I heard someone say to me, *"Go into the backwaters of every territory, and with your justice, bring the Goddess."*

The words were still ringing in my mind as David and I crawled into the back of his brother Tom's four-wheel-drive truck. Daniel, who was at thirteen taller and bigger than I am, sat up front, and Tom's girlfriend Gina, petite and sparkly-eyed, squeezed in back with David and me. We headed up to Dolly Sodds, a mountain whose name no one ever did explain to me. We drove around hairpin turns overlooking deep valleys, trying not to fall into one another. The words faded, forgotten, as I became uncomfortably engrossed in the exchanges between David and Gina. Each time either of them said something to the other across my line of vision, I couldn't help but notice the light in their eyes, couldn't help but hear the smile in their voices. I tried to ease back out of their way. I tried to peer through the small back window at the tops of trees passing below us. I began wishing I could just shrink into the crack of the seat and fall out the bottom of the car, an unnoticed pebble bouncing off the narrow road, down, down, down the mountainside into oblivion.

Our small party leaned into the wind, took in the view, and picked huckleberries. Whenever David and Gina gravitated toward one another, I meandered off in some other direction, in such a state of secret torment that I was sure I was noticeably reeking of self-consciousness, and that heat waves of insecurity were visibly rising from my hunched shoulders. Wasn't Tom worried about his girlfriend finding his brother attractive? Wasn't David noticing that I was feeling pathetically abandoned? Hot flashes sent their neon red rashes up my turkey-skin neck. Liver spots I'd never noticed before jumped up and cackled at me hideously.

Back at our campsite after dark, David and Daniel and I unpacked the chicken hot dogs and rolls and mustard. Before reaching for the dead branches we'd piled nearby, I propped a handful of dry twigs over some crumpled paper in the low fire barrel. David smirked. "You call that firewood?" He was teasing. That frown was just part of the tease, but it was a *frown*, damn it, not a sparkle, not a smile, not a glow of warm happy light. I got up to spear my dinner onto a pronged twig and smacked him on the butt in passing, a little harder than I'd intended. He didn't say anything. I managed to swallow a few bites of my blackened hot dog, and sat down on the picnic table bench next to Daniel.

"Hey, you can't sit here, crazy woman," Daniel teased.

I got up and went to the other side of the table. I was in

one foul mood and I was about to spill over and douse the fire of a perfectly lovely evening. I stood up. David had been watching me. There was a question on his face. It hurt to see it there. "I'm going to take a walk," I said, my voice cracking, and I left without looking back.

That's what I wanted to do, I told myself as I sat under a tree on the other side of the playground, in the dark. Walk away from it all and never look back. And before I could finish imagining what it would be like not to have David to snuggle with every night, my eyes were flooding, my throat was aching with the need to cry out, and I bawled. I sobbed. I was six. I was crying for the last time for my father to put his arms around me, and then I would never cry again. I would just tough it out through all my teenage years. I would just endure his remoteness, his perfectionism, and his preoccupation. I would never cry for anyone to put his arms around me again. Only I was crying now. I wanted David to hold me. I wanted him to need me and love me and want me. Tears flooded down and joined the goopy drippings from my nose and I had no tissues and BB's were probably *pouring* out of my elbows . . . .

A sudden huffing snort shot through the darkness. The silhouette of a motionless deer stood against the pale night sky.

Go into the backwaters of every territory, and with your justice, bring the Goddess.

I pulled the six-year-old inside me from the backwaters of my emotional history, let her finish wiping her nose on my sleeve, and stood up.

I knew what I had to say to David.

I walked back along the road past darkened recreational vehicles, stepping off to one side as the headlights of a car approached me. They aimed right at me, and David said through the open window, "Where have you been? It's been lonely without you."

"I'll meet you back at the campsite."

"Don't you want to ride with me?"

I got in. "I'm sorry," I began, tears of self-pity welling up as soon as the words were out of my mouth. "I didn't want to spoil the evening for you and Daniel. I was just going through some stuff . . . "

"You can talk to me about it."

"No, it was just dumb stuff." I knew what I had to say, but, oh, it was going to be so hard to say it.

"I guess my stupid sense of humor didn't help."

"How could you have known?"

"I walked out here twice looking for you."

The tears spilled over.

He took me into his arms.

"David, I don't ever want to be in the way of you exchanging good energy with anyone else the way you and Gina were doing today. I want to get out of the way and let that happen, but I need to know that you care about me, too, because if you don't, then I just want you to say so and get it over with, because it would be so hard to go on without you, but I could do it, even though I don't want to lose you, and I'm sorry I need you so much, but sometimes I'm not sure you care . . . " I blubbered out all over his chest.

"I'm sorry," he said quietly. "I do care."

"But maybe you'd be better off with someone else who makes you light up . . . "

"*You* make me light up. Where else would I find anyone with your personality? Who else in the world has a personality like yours?"

When he pulled the van into the slot beside our campsite, Daniel came to the window.

As I rolled down the window I said, "I'm sorry if I spoiled the evening, Daniel. I just needed to figure some things out for myself. We'll be done talking soon."

"That's okay," he said. He looked at me gently, and then walked back to his tent.

"Daniel and I both need to know we're special to you, David. Sometimes we don't know that. You get remote sometimes. What have you been going through?"

He told me. He was feeling stressed because he wasn't making enough money yet with the Web site. He wasn't feeling good about himself in his own way, wasn't meeting his own expectations of himself. He didn't even try to explain why Gina's attentiveness had been a welcome distraction. I understood without him saying so that being found attractive was an upper.

I had done it. I had said it. *I need you.*

And he had given me what I'd needed. Himself.

I wanted our next evening, our last evening, to be one of family harmony, but Daniel had isolated himself in his tent with his Final Fantasy Seven notebook and his headphones. David and I sat and gazed into the campfire, still not completely in synch with one another. The woods were dark. I wondered if the deer were watching us.

. . . and with your justice, bring the Goddess.

I was still feeling so wretchedly vulnerable. How could I bring the Goddess into this situation? Goddess of home and hearth and family . . . I had ruined that wonderful feeling of family we'd been building . . .

"Let's go tell Daniel what a good kid he is, you want to?" I finally suggested.

David got up and lit the way with his flashlight.

"Daniel, thanks for being such a great camper," I groped for the right words, aiming them toward the silhouette in the zipped-up tent. Daniel answered with a circle of light from his flashlight against the red nylon door.

"You're a good son, Daniel," David said to the tent, touching the circle of light with the beam from his own flashlight. "I wouldn't want to go camping with any other kid."

"Thanks, Dad," came from inside the red glow, and it was truly meant.

"My flashlight is kissing your flashlight," David pointed out with a smile in his voice.

"Pervert!"

"Goodnight, Daniel."

"Goodnight, Dad. Goodnight, Lesta. Thank you."

I woke up to the sound of something crunching loudly right outside the tent. I was alone. What *was* that strange sound? I unzipped the door, just enough to look out.

Our favorite deer was eating the corn chips David had trailed to a pile in front of our tent. She poked her head in and licked her nose at me. Behind her David was smiling. I could see it was going to be a beautiful day.

33

Dreams Speak

Who *was* that man?

I didn't want to wake up from the dream I'd had on the morning of June 22, 1989. A tall, heavyset Native American, his dull black shoulder-length hair worn down, had put his large hands on my shoulders, looked deeply into my eyes, and, without words, both beseeched and promised me: there was something I could do for him, and there was something he could do for me.

But what, I wondered. What can I do for this man whose face is haunting me, hour after hour, all day long? Needing to know more, I stilled myself into a meditation that evening. He appeared to me again, his mouth turned down in sorrow, his wide jaw set with clenched resolve, and waved his hand toward the history of his ancestry. Under the branches of an immense conifer, a huge silvery bear lumbers to the crest of a boulder. Beneath the imposing animal crouches a wiry gray-haired man in a breechcloth, armed with a spear that snaps into splinters as the bear, with startling speed and agility, descends and attacks. With blood streaking from the gashes on his limbs, the warrior thrusts his hand into the snarling, frothing jaws, his arm disappearing up to his shoulder as his fist jams into the throat of the beast. The bear, clawing and reeling, unable to dislodge its opponent, stumbles and finally slumps to the ground, choking to death. The warrior, during his long season of recovery, loses his hand, but gains the spirit of the bear and hands it down through many generations to the man in my dream.

What does this vision have to do with how much I am aching to fulfill some mysterious promise?

I begin to look through some books on Native Americans, longing to find some answer, paging through photographs, until I stop and gasp, my heart starting to hammer at the sight of his face. It's him! He actually existed? Who is he?

Heavyset, wide-jawed, shoulder-length hair worn open, the same eyes that had looked into mine in my dream: he was the Kiowa chief Satanta, or Set'Tainte, which translates as White Bear.

Satanta, I read, was a powerful and rebellious chief during the 1870s when the Kiowa, Cheyenne, Comanche, Arapaho, and other tribes were being rounded up and confined to reservations. He was clever, spoke well, and had several wives and many children; he had compassion and fury, he killed and evaded the white soldiers again and again, but he was finally captured. He took to drinking while imprisoned in the penitentiary at Huntsville, Texas, and finally leaped to his death from a second story window in 1878. His remains were later moved to Fort Sill. He is still revered by the Kiowa.

I was at a loss. What was it I could do for a Kiowa chief who had died a hundred and eleven years ago? Had Satanta actually appeared to me, or was it some strange coincidence that I had dreamed of him and then found his photograph? I thought about how drawn I was to the Plains Indians. My first drawings, which my mother saved from when I was five years old, were of tepees and men with feathers on horses. What was my connection to the Kiowa? What was I being called to do?

I almost wanted to give up trying to figure it all out, but I wasn't allowed to forget the dream. Every few days for weeks after, something would happen to make me remember it. One afternoon my son came home from school and casually plopped his books onto the couch. One of them fell open. I sat down next to it, slightly stunned. On the page at which the book had fallen open was a photograph of Satanta. I looked at the cover of the book—a tenth grade American Literature textbook. Next to the photograph was a speech Satanta had given to the white authorities, about how much he loved the land, loved the freedom of roaming the land, how he would never willingly give up that freedom because it meant life to him.

I had more dreams. In one, I was walking through a forest and I came upon a bear, buried up to its neck. Only its head was still visible, and it gazed at me, with that same longing in its eyes, as if to tell me there was not much time left before it could no longer communicate with me.

On my birthday, two months after the initial dream, I felt compelled to clean out a closet. I pulled out a long-forgotten cardboard box I had stashed there over five years before. Among other keepsakes that my mother had passed on to me from her father was a leather-bound book with the word *Autographs* inscribed in gold on the cover. It was so old and fragile that the pages were in danger of falling apart. Very carefully, I opened it. On every page was a watercolor drawing. Tepees surrounded by women in long dresses. Men on horseback shooting arrows into bison or antelope on the run. Chiefs in body-length feathered headdresses. Games being played with sticks and balls. Page after page of Plains Indian life scenes. The drawings were signed. Nacoista. Koba. Buffalo Meat.

Etahdleuh. Making Medicine. White Man. Cohoe. Holding my breath, I turned back to the first page. Handwritten in pencil were about thirty names, listed under the headings Kiowa, Cheyenne, Comanche, and Arapaho. All the names of the artists were included, and there were others. Lone Wolf. Howling Wolf. One of the names was White Bear.

I had found my answer.

This precious record had ended up in the hands of a white woman descended from a European man who had acquired it from another white woman in Massachusetts in June of 1946. Where else it had been on its journey might remain a mystery, but its origin, I was to discover, was Fort Marion, Florida. Prisoners captured in Texas in 1875 were transported by train to Fort Marion, where they were "encouraged" to absorb themselves into the white culture. A Captain Pratt, whose intentions were to be helpful, taught the men English and gave them art supplies and told them to do what they had never needed to do before, claim authorship by signing their works, so that they might make a living by selling them. How many of these books were produced, or have survived, I do not know, but I was holding one of them, and I finally knew what I could do for Satanta. I could return this book of beautiful watercolor drawings to its rightful heirs—his descendants.

Further research revealed that Satanta had not been among the prisoners sent to Fort Marion; the White Bear listed in the book was an Arapaho, and not the man in my dream. But the director of the Oklahoma Historical Society was in contact with a 92-year-old Kiowa elder, Parker McKenzie (who has recently celebrated his 100th birthday in Carnegie, Oklahoma), a descendent of one of the prisoners, Double Vision, a friend of Satanta's.

Mr. McKenzie's knobby fingers turned the pages with trembling care as he studied scene after scene of a lifestyle lost to his people. I wondered, as I witnessed his quiet pain, if I had done the right thing. When he agreed to hand the book over to the director of the Historical Society, to be kept on permanent loan in controlled museum conditions, I was disappointed. Despite the fact that art historians might better preserve it for future generations, I had hoped that it could be kept in the small museum in Carnegie, where the Kiowa community could view it as their own. I left Mr. McKenzie's little clapboard house feeling I had failed to fulfill my mission. The precious book of paintings was once again in the hands of white people.

I had no further communications from Satanta.

Seven years passed.

I had begun my career as an artist. After having had a few successful shows, I was considering the possibility of getting my work published. I sent photographs of my paintings to several book publishing companies, hoping to be commissioned for a book-jacket illustration, but there were no positive responses.

And then, one afternoon, a friend of a friend called and asked me if I would be interested in making an illustration for a book jacket.

"Oh, wow, yes, definitely!" Something inside me perked its ears. "What's the book about?"

"It's entitled *Dreamspeak*. It's a vocabulary of dream images, information that's been channeled through the author from a spirit called White Bear."

There was something I could do for him, and there was something he could do for me.

Even though I never found out anything more about the spirit who had channeled the book *Dreamspeak,* and even though I doubt that it was the same White Bear, I do not doubt now that Satanta had something to do with that job being offered to me. It was my first published artwork, but not my last.

Exactly ten years to the day after I had found the book of watercolors in my closet—two days ago—I received a letter from an associate professor of art history in a southwestern university. She had had the privilege of examining the book of watercolors kept in the museum of the Oklahoma Historical

Society, and she would appreciate any further information on it. I sent her what information I had, including the story of my dream. I wished her well in her research and thanked her for reminding me of how inspired I had been to learn more about the history of the book and its creators. As I concluded my letter, it occurred to me that perhaps that beautiful and sad collection of artworks is one of the ways in which more white people will be awakened to the tragedy, the talents, and the enduring spirit of the Native Americans.

I suspect that this story is not yet finished.

But I have already learned one thing for sure.

Dreams speak.

34

Pink

David dreamed that I handed him a piece of paper edged with perforated strips of holes, the kind used in continuous-feed printers, except that instead of being white, it was pink. As he tore off the strips of holes, he noticed that the figure of a large sum of money had been printed on the pink paper. It seemed I'd given him a receipt, or a promise, the first of more to come. He interpreted the dream: pink represents love. He was accepting from me a large and continuous amount of loving support.

We've been cleaning and repairing the space a half-level down from his apartment in order to bring to fruition a dream he'd all but given up on. He has wanted to open a store for many years, but somehow the space would get clogged with friends' storage or there wouldn't be enough time or money to finish the ceiling. Two years' worth of roadblocks between him and his goal was what we were clearing away so we could open up a Visionary Art and Gift Gallery that would substantiate and supplement his online store. Before we could arrange his crystals, wands, pyramids, books, meditational music CD's, my paintings and prints, and whatever else would serve to uplift and enlighten our visitors, we still needed to get rid of several of his acquired auction leftovers.

"What should I do with this rocking chair?" he wondered out loud. "Maybe just keep it in here," he decided. "Maybe someone will want to buy it." He vacuumed around it. "I'm not going to need these five sheets of drywall. They're the wrong thickness." He took one outside, leaned it against the railing of the deck, and scrawled "Free" on it. "Maybe someone will go by and just happen to need some drywall," he shrugged.

Angel came downstairs from the apartment, wearing a loose, bright pink dress. "This is a really good location for a store," she told me. "People are always watching to see what's going on here. And you're doing it right," she checked the business hours sign I was filling in. "Being open only from Friday through Monday. That way you aren't so tied to it that it takes over your life." She had nothing but good things to say to us. She was pleased, it was apparent, that we would finally be around more, even if it wouldn't be at night. Since Dan had been taking her to a spiritual group meeting every week, she hadn't been complaining of intruders, although she still pushed a dresser against the door after dark. So when David told her he was installing a lock between the apartment and the store, she was nothing but happy.

We hadn't told her that she'd been one of the deciding factors in going ahead with the store. Whether we opened the store or not, we'd be paying the rent as long as she needed a place to stay, so we might as well do two good things at once, one for her and one for us.

How good it was for David to materialize his dream was obvious. It was making sense to him that it hadn't happened two years ago. Coming home from painting houses had left him so exhausted that all he'd wanted to do was to sit in front of his computer. It had taken him two years of lonely evenings to build his hundred-some-page Web site. If he hadn't mentioned his Web site in his personals ad, I might never have answered it. If I hadn't come into his life, he would never have had the encouragement he needed to take down the ladders and put up a sign that says "Open."

How good it was for me to have what I could call my own gallery hit home only after I stepped back and surveyed the walls, hung with seventeen of my paintings. And there were still shelves that needed sculptures . . . bookends . . . decorative boxes . . . !

David's neighbor, Louis, who'd been working on his van for several weeks, stopped in to give an update on the progress of the fuel tank. After looking all over for a used one, he'd had to buy a new one after all. That's what was taking him so long, he explained, but he would have it by Tues ay. "Oh, by the way," Louis remembered, "my sister peeked in the window when she saw you were finally getting the store ready to open, and she wants to know if you want to sell that chair." David's eyebrows went up. He nodded, trying not to smile. "Oh, and, hey," Louis added, "I'll be happy to take that drywall off your hands." The smile broadened.

Louis hefted a sheet onto his shoulder, despite the fact that his pinky finger was throbbing. Someone had dropped a fork-lift load on it, and it was swollen to twice its normal size. After he had carried the last sheet of drywall next door, Louis followed David back into the store space. "Hey, man," he looked around, "what kind of rock you got for good luck?"

David shook his head. He'd been getting e-mail requests asking what mineral was good for what problem, and it took him quite some time either to look it up or to still himself long enough to get the information from either a spirit guide or a mineral spirit. I could see him not wanting to mislead his neighbor with a careless answer.

"What kind of good luck do you need?" I asked, hoping to be helpful. "For money? For healing? For love?"

"Oh, it's not for me, it's for my daughter. I don't want her thinking I'm a bad father, just because I won't let her go to just anybody's house. Hey, if I don't know those people, then the answer is No, not till I meet them. She's not too crazy about that. She doesn't get it. I do it because I love her and want to protect her, you know?"

"Oh, then what you need is some rose quartz," I suggested, pulling a smooth pink stone from one of the paper bags on the counter, hoping that David would pick up on my lead. He knows so much more than I do about such things. I just know that pink represents love.

"That's right," David piped up. "Pink is love energy. And you better give her an amethyst for good measure." He pulled out a tumbled stone from another paper bag.

"Oh, this is great. This is great," Louis weighed the gifts in his palm. "Man, this finger is really throbbing."

It had been a long time since David had done any healing. He used to heal sickness and pain with different light tools and minerals, depending on how he was instructed by the spirit guides working through him, but he hadn't felt healed enough himself from the past few years of distraction and discouragement to attempt much healing on anyone else, so I'm not sure what prompted me to wonder out loud, "David, could you do some Reiki on Louis?"

"Reiki?" he frowned. He doesn't see the point of using a Japanese word for what he calls universal light energy. "Sure. I'll get my rake."

"This isn't going to hurt, is it?" Louis was apprehensive.

David looked into my eyes. The way we've been looking into one another's eyes lately has been full of communication on many levels.

He told Louis to wait a minute, and he went upstairs and

came back down with an orange calcite pyramid in his hand. The spirit of that mineral had informed him that it could heal certain kinds of pain; he had used it successfully many times in the past.

I walked outside and sat in my van to do a little writing.

Five minutes later, Louis walked by, fairly humming to himself, bouncing along, swinging his arms, no longer protectively guarding his little finger.

David locked up the store and climbed into the driver's seat. Light was shining from his eyes. He talked all the way back to my place. Not only had the pain disappeared from Louis's finger, but from a sore area on his leg as well. Louis was going to bring his wife over. And a friend. For healing. He wanted to buy the piece of orange calcite; he'd gotten a really good feeling from it. David gave it to him to take along. They could worry about paying each other later, when the work on the van was finished. Once the word spread, David said excitedly, people would come to the store to get a healing, and if they wanted to buy something, great, but just doing the healing, that's what he's really been wanting to do. . . .

I sat and listened the whole way home, smiling.

David bounded upstairs to answer his e-mail requests for spiritual guidance.

I went outside. Rinsing out a litter box with the hose, next to the no-longer-used little duck pond, I noticed the water suddenly turning pink. Hot glowing pink. So pink my arms were pink in the glow. What?

I looked up. It wasn't the pond water that was pink. The pond was only reflecting the sky. The clouds, dispersed at just the right altitude, were bathing the entire sky in a radiant, creamy pink, so pervasively rosy that the air was pink, the field was pink, my hands were pink.

"David!" I yelled up at the open window. "Look! Everything is pink!"

"Are you on drugs?" he yelled back.

He came outside and we sat and looked at everything

awash in wondrous, living, loving pink. I thought of the pink receipt in his dream, the pink dress Angel had worn as she praised our efforts, the pink stone Louis was going to give his daughter, and I grinned at Mama Terra, adding her own grand finale to a perfectly pink day.

35

Whenever the Spirit Moves You

About ten years ago, one of my son's friends, Rena, a soft-spoken, gentle soul, stopped in to talk with me about a young man she'd been very much in love with. She couldn't make any sense of his suicide. She herself had no more desire to participate in life. There was still not the faintest glimmer of hope or understanding in her eyes when she left. Because I myself was losing someone I loved, I had hoped to convince us both that there was something greater we could count on and surrender to, but my words had sounded hollow.

As I rinsed out my coffee cup, wondering how I could have opened Rena to the presence of Spirit, I had the strange sensation that I needed to go outside to find something. Something was pulling at me. I walked down the driveway, almost following a scent in the air, or turning my head to catch a sound, but it wasn't a scent or a sound, although it directed me as if it were. I turned down the road . . . now turn right here, it tugged, toward the pond. As I passed the tall spruces, the sensation went off like a Geiger counter on my left. Under the trees? I pushed aside the low branches, and there on the needled carpet lay a candle. A bright red, shiny new, tapered candle. How did a candle get there? This candle is a message, I heard myself thinking, and I will know what the message is within three days.

During the next two days, I was helped to let go of the person who was leaving my life by a dream of release, a phone call of gentle resolution, and an invitation to attend an opening. I paid attention to each of them as markers of transition, and because the candle had alerted me to do so, I decided to leave it, in case anyone else was drawn to it for their own message, at the campsite in the woods where my son Eric was planning to have a Friday night party.

On Saturday morning, Rena stopped in again to share photos of her lost love. It had been three weeks since his incomprehensible act of finality, and she still felt numb.

"Rena, if you listen to the messages that come from all around you and within you, you'll begin to understand," I was finally able to assure her with conviction. "There is something greater than us that wants to lead us into our own best directions, if we let it. If you open up to it, you'll be given the answers you need." I told how I'd been led to find the red candle, and how it had helped me notice that what I was leaving behind was making room for something new.

"It's funny it was a red candle," she said, her soft eyes wanting to believe me. "There was a red candle at the party last night, and two of the guys and me all held our hands together and dripped wax all over them until they were stuck together, and one of the guys laughed and said, 'Bonded for life!'"

"Rena! That was it! That was your message! That was the same red candle! I left it there yesterday, and now I know why.

You were being told it's time to bond yourself to life again, your friends are there for you, and Spirit is with you, making sure you know that." A spark lit up her eyes as she let my words sink in. The spark grew into a glow—she looked surrounded by love—and for the first time in three weeks, she smiled.

A year later, Rena stopped in to tell me she was in love. She'd never been so happy. After she left, I took a walk down to the pond, full of gratitude for the way life had opened up for her and was opening up for me. To my surprise, I found two red candles in the woods.

Yesterday I was supposed to be at a certain place at a certain time, but something was pulling at me to go somewhere. I drove past my brother's house. Here? No . . . where to? On my way to wherever it was, I passed the yellow gate. I decided to stop and collect the filled trash bag, take it up the hill to the end of my driveway, and try to make my appointment after all. As I was relining the can with a new bag, someone came walking out of the woods toward me.

"Hey, I really like your sign," she said, placing two empty bottles into the can.

Wow, I thought, someone else is cleaning up the litter.

"I used to come here when I was little," she told me. "I'm just in the area for a few days, visiting my dad, and this is one of the places I knew I wanted to see again. There's not nearly as much trash as there used to be. People must be feeling reminded to be respectful because of your sign."

Oh! *This* is where I was being drawn! To be told my sign is working!

"I'm on my way to Alaska," she continued. She'd just gotten out of a bad relationship, she told me, and she wished she didn't feel like all men were awful, but she'd given up hope of ever meeting a man who was easy to be with.

Easy to be with? Oh my dear! "I felt exactly the same way a couple of years ago," I told her. "But five months ago I met a man who is exactly what you described—easy to be with." I told her how David and I had met, and how many of our areas of interest overlap, especially the spiritual.

"Oh, this meeting was meant to take place!" she exclaimed. "A spiritual man! You have just given me so much hope! Thank you so much!"

We shared a warm hug.

I was forty-five minutes late for my meeting.

So was the other person.

Whenever the Spirit moves you, for your sake and others', be moved!

36

As You Will

During the drought, did people in this area pray for rain? If they did, their prayers were answered, big time. Hurricane Floyd brought enough rain in two days to make up for two months of none.

Last week I delivered a piece of artwork to a friend in New York City. I do not like going into the city, I do not like being in the city, and I do not like trying to get out of the city, so my expectations for the day could be summed up in one word: frazzling.

Beware your expectations, for they shall be fulfilled.

On the way there, already eager to get the day over with before it had begun, I didn't even notice that I was passing traffic on a long downhill slope as if traffic had come to a crawl.

When I saw the police car and glanced down at my speedometer, I rolled my eyes and pulled over as soon as my rearview mirror showed the cop pulling onto the highway. He didn't even have to flash me. He did anyway, of course. He handed me the $150 speeding ticket (ouch!) and wished me Godspeed. Mm-hmm.

Okay, so I'm only twenty minutes late.

I turn on the ignition and discover that my driver's side window has decided at this very moment to quit working. It goes down. It does not go back up. It gasps its final death rattle and stays down there inside that door and isn't about to come back up for anything, I can tell. I can tell what kind of a day it's going to be, too, as my hair whips across my face and as I breathe in those tunnel fumes and get blasted with the over-stimulation of the city sounds and smells I was dreading. The routes across Central Park to the East Side are all closed for the day. Okay, so I'm another half an hour behind schedule. Fine.

I double park outside my friend's apartment, and run in to ask the doorman to buzz her. We leave the delicate sculpture with him (yikes) while we go find a place to park. Oops, not down this street. Everybody back up and lay on your horn like an idiot. The truck in front of me can't get through the double-parking. What, pay $30 to park underground for two hours? I don't *think* so. I leave my van beside a meter, unlocked. What would be the point? That window is so *glaringly* open. This is just great. I surround the van with a prayer of white light and a cloak of invisibility.

I do not like New York with spam. I do not like New York one gram.

The doorman had carried the sculpture off and locked it in a closet. When we got it up to my friend's apartment, we discovered that it was *all bent out of shape,* like myself by the time I hurried back to my van before the meter ran out. Didn't I leave my van right there?

Oh, yes, there it is, almost invisible . . . and, miraculously, untouched.

Aha, take note, woman, the one positive intent of the day resulted in a positive outcome.

And lest I forget this noteworthy message . . . Yesterday as I was driving to the frame shop, I noticed that my wiper blades were leaving smudges on the windshield. Oh great, I muttered to myself. One more thing. After that speeding ticket, after getting my window repaired, and finally getting the oil changed . . . what, now I need new wiper blades? I'm in the middle of this negative tirade and I don't even notice what I'm doing until suddenly the wipers stop dead in their tracks, straight up and down. No more smudges, baby, just big splatters of rain all over the windshield.

"Oh, no! I'm sorry!" I yell. "I'm so glad I have wiper blades! I don't care about a little smudge. I'm so happy to have blades that work!"

They sit there in their vertical position, not responding to the switch, and the windshield gets harder to see through. "Thank you for your reminder. I love you, car. I love you, universe. You're right, I shouldn't complain, I'm so fortunate. Thank you." I'm rolling my eyes at myself, laughing, relaxing, enjoying my new attitude, and not even minding that I'll have to stop at the next gas station . . . when all of the sudden, the wiper blades start working again. Swish, swot, swish, swot, what you wish is what you got.

And the rain comes down, in sheets, flooding our too eager prayers back at us.

It's not a new lesson to be learned. It's an old one to be unlearned, so that we can revitalize ourselves with the awesome power of our birthright—the knowledge that all the universe ever wants to say to us is Okay. This is what you expect? Okay. This is what you intend? Okay! This is how you will filter the magnificent energy flowing through you and from you, into this outcome? Okay. This is the way in which your commitment to beauty and joy and abundance will draw Heaven to Earth? Okay!

37

Do Nothing

Okay, it's time to have another argument with myself.

Or, I could start this chapter with, Dear Mother of God, universe, infinite source of wisdom and love, Great Spirit, I seek an answer that is so far beyond my comprehension at the moment that any name I can think of to invoke a response will be added to the list, not out of reverence, but out of desperation. God! Allah! Goddess! Higher Self? Help!

The situation that is keeping me awake all night, that has me opening my eyes onto the Pleiades peeking through my window in the wee hours of the morning, that has located itself in a throbbing tooth, is one that is way too common, at least in my experiences on the planet, and I don't understand why or what to do about it.

I am witnessing a young member of this society suffering from constant pain, from suppressed rage that manifests as depression and physical incapacitation. I see the cause as an "older" (using the term here in human years, not soul years) member of this society, who, by definition of parenthood, has the "right" to determine Johnny's reality for him, and that reality is counter to his nature, his need to be recognized as a self-sovereign individual, and his well-being. I see the distorted reality of the parent not only being imposed on Johnny, but also being used to justify an energy drain that threatens to waste his life force. I see one human being who is pained, powerless, and unhappy, unconsciously creating desperation, helplessness, and misery in another in order to successfully maintain the illusion that there is no other way to live.

Aaarrruuugh!

I thought I had finally come to understand the wisdom of totally trusting the universe to respond in the best possible way to human intentions. David's brother has asked if he can move into David's apartment, which would be a great situation for both of them, because they would be sharing both the rent and the two rooms between the apartment and the store for workspace and classes. But of course this can't happen until Angel, who isn't paying any rent, moves out. With a patience I'd call stubborn if I didn't trust his wisdom, David explained that while it seems things are moving in a good direction, he cannot insist that she move out. She has already suffered too many losses and abandonments: the death of a husband, the death of her best friend, and the years-long estrangement of her children.

He has been hoping to provide her with a place and time to do some healing, and he doesn't want to undermine eight months of respite with one blow of rejection, no matter how much better it would be for him to have her leave. He might be the only person on the planet who can ensure that she doesn't end up in a mental institution, and he would rather live with the inconvenience than force her toward such a hell.

However, he went on, he does imagine that she would be happier living with someone who wanted to be with her than living alone. So the prayer he offers up to the universe is not that his life be made easier for him, but that Angel's life be made easier for her, however that needs to happen. And then he lets go of the outcome. He's okay with whatever the outcome will be.

If he's provided with support, with enough money to continue to pay the rent for Angel, and she needs him to do that, fine. If he isn't, if he can't, then whatever happens next is whatever the universe is manifesting toward the most needed end. He simply regards Angel with divine love, acts as a conscious channel of love flowing toward her, and makes no judgments or decisions concerning how love will act on her behalf. When he had finished fully explaining his view, not only did I understand the enlightened consciousness of his thinking, I felt myself sharing it. I felt myself loving everything just the way it is. I trusted everything to continue to be the way it needs to be, given what we are moving from and what we are moving toward.

And then I ran into this other situation.

And I know, I know—the two souls who are caught in this life-and-death struggle, who are both in a vicious cycle of pain and medication and symptomatic responses and unmet needs, have on some level chosen this experience to live out who they are, and their journeys are going to be as drawn out as it takes for them to resolve whatever they have to resolve.

But I want to scream!

I want to say, look at what you are doing, you, you parasite you! You are feeding on your child's life energy! You are pretending to love him while you wrap him up in your spider web of delusion! You are manipulating and controlling the joy right out of his being! Get with the program! Get a life!

I also wanted to scream when I found out that my ex-husband has an alcoholic girlfriend who is pregnant with his child. Oh, God, another miserable human being in the making, the least trusting part of me thought, shaking her head in dismay. The most trusting part of me hopes that this might be his chance for a new life. This might be the son he's always wanted. This child might give him a reason to heal himself and grow into the best possible version of himself, or at least to redeem himself in his own eyes, or to reconnect with his daughters, who would love their sibling. So I activate the most trusting prayers, and in my own small way, act as a channel for love. Please let this be the beginning of something wonderful. But then, I have to detach myself from the outcome, don't I? Because this little me really doesn't know what those souls are all about, or what love will decide is the best route for them to take.

I can detach from them, no problem, having already acted powerfully on my own behalf to detach from him.

But Johnny has appealed to me for help. And, so, hey up there, am I just a witness? Am I an angel assigned to touch lives? Am I a helpless bystander? Am I a Light worker?

You are a self-sovereign, self-creating being. You can create your reality around this any way you want to.

That's what I want to tell Johnny.

Then do.

But what effect will a few words every now and then have on years of misguided information?

What effect did they have on other young people who came into your reality and appealed to you for help?

As much as they wanted them to.

So he has to want your words and your help.

And he does.

So he will make use of them as much as he wants to.

But still, that means I can't snap my fingers and say presto, do this with your life right now and all your pain will go away. And the reason I can't is because I'm not the parent. I can see a solution, but the parent doesn't agree. The parent is attached to the reality that's been created for and by the two of them.

Aha. Who has participated in creating their reality?

Both of them, but only because Johnny has been forced to! That's why he's silently enraged and overtly depressed!

Because he sees nothing ahead of him but more control over his reality than he has any power to influence.

So you are buying into his being helpless?

Oh.

If he wants to live according to his own nature, he will.

If he doesn't want to, he'll give up?

That is up to him.

But aren't we all in this together?

If you feel so strongly that you want to respond to his call for help, then do.

I see. What about staying detached from the outcome?

If that works to keep you peaceful and focused and generating good energy into the atmosphere, then use that method. If you get frustrated because you aren't reaching the goal you want to reach, and your frustration generates negative energy into the situation, you will only be interfering with your own best purpose. If you intend a positive outcome, without defining it precisely, you give yourself more room to appreciate whatever progress is being made instead of measuring it against the finish line, which might be further off than you want it to be at this moment. It could also be closer than you think. But looking at it takes your eyes off looking at what is right in front of you.

Looking at what is right in front of me shows me a dangerously unhappy human being.

Dangerous meaning he could end this particular lifetime in order to bring home a message to those around him?

Oh, God. Are you trying to remind me that our lives are so much bigger than this immediate suffering?

I'm trying to remind you that there are many reasons for things to be the way they are. I'm trying to remind you that you are right now creating your own reality. You can be distressed about something that might or might not be what you think it is. Your distress might drive you to make changes. Or you can change your distress. All of these and more are choices available to you.

So I can't call upstairs and say, hey, this is a mess down here, what do I do about it?

Sure you can.

Okay. This is a mess down here. What do I do about it? And don't say anything I want to! I want a specific answer! Don't ask *me* what I want to do about it! I want you to *tell* me what to do about it!

All I can tell you is that whatever you want to do about it will be fine to do.

You don't judge me. I already get that.

Whatever you want to do about it is what I, too, want done.

I want these two people to be helped forward, away from pain and delusion and into health and consciousness. I want to be of assistance if my assistance is received, and to trust that if it isn't, there will be other ways for this to happen.

This is a given. In Time and No-Time, these two individuals, all individuals, will be and are already whole and holy.

All that is well and good if You're floating around with all these galaxies inside You, living in the Great Big Now, but I'm down here where things hurt sometimes, and I just don't want to see any more unnecessary pain. Don't You want all these little parts of You to be healthy? Don't You want to be filled with our joy?

Although peace and joy are on your mind right now, the greatest gift you can ask of me, like the greatest gift your children asked of you, is freedom of self-expression and self-sovereignty. Remember how long it has taken you to free yourself from feeling responsible for the outcomes that your loved ones must choose for themselves. Allow other souls to take their own time to discover this same freedom, and truly trust both them and me, and you will have your peace and your joy, which I welcome from you as much as I welcome your concern. Your desires have been heard. Your wish to be a channel of love has been fulfilled. Simply love. Love them where they are, for it is where they need to be. Show them where else they can go, and love them even if they don't go there. Know that you are loved, no matter what.

I still want them to be happier than they are.

Sometimes the greatest happiness is discovered through the greatest trials.

I understand that. I do understand that. The strength and the humbling, the ability to surrender and the power to act, the evaluation of what is truly worthwhile, the initiative to go forward with less trepidation and more of a sense of adventure, I understand how those evolve from testing ourselves, from making it through the rough parts of the road.

So you would not want to rob others of their triumphs over difficulties.

Which is another way of saying, okay, it hurts, it's hard, but sometimes that's what is needed to urge us into a better place.

A different place. Better if it is felt as better.

And that is up to each of us to discover—what feels better. Okay. I guess.

I finish this conversation with my tooth still throbbing, as it has since the middle of the night, signifying to me a serious energy block in my sense of personal power and my ability to digest what I am taking in. Fawni comes in to chat.

We remember together that the best things have come true every time we simply expected them to, without doubts, worries, fears, and impatience.

The September after Fawni graduated from high school brought with it a restlessness for involvement in something purposeful. She didn't want to go to college, so she asked the universe to give her direction. A few days later, an interesting brochure arrived in the mail. Massage classes were being offered by a healing arts academy located four miles from our home.

Within seven months Fawni became an accredited massage therapist and was earning thirty-five dollars an hour doing something she loved doing so much that she has continued to take classes, moving from deep muscle massage into energy work. Recently, as she was applying her newly learned polarity techniques to a classmate, she felt someone rest their hands on her shoulders from behind, and she heard a whispered, "Yes, this is what you are meant to be doing." A rush of heightened energy surged through her. She glanced around. No one was behind her. She has found her passion and her purpose, and she has been given confirmation of support and guidance from the Other Side.

By the time Fawni goes back downstairs to fix dinner, my tooth has stopped throbbing. I have regained my patience and my personal power. I can take in what I need to. And it is patience and detachment that I bring to the conversation I have with Johnny's parent. And so I am able to hear, from behind the façade of control and helplessness, a true glimmer of hope, a willingness to consider options, a need for change and for everyone's best interests to be kept in mind.

Meanwhile, David comes home and reports that his brother has decided to move into his apartment even though Angel is still there. When she got upset that he didn't confer with her on this decision, he reminded her that she has been wanting to move on, and that this might be a good time to do so.

I think I'm getting it. Don't do, just be; don't work so hard toward a desired end, just *see* it. It doesn't have to be that hard; everything *will* change, with or without my determined effort to *make* it change. Or, as Lao-Tzu so succinctly put it, *Do nothing, and nothing will remain undone.*

38

On Another Level

I know I'm not the only one who's ever felt this way.

I might as well be, at least for today, floating untethered in space, a lost soul who's up and died and doesn't know where home is.

As lonely as it is out here, I look down and wonder why anyone would ever go back to that planet. The inhabitants are insane. When you arrive, they slap you, burn your eyes, stick needles into you, and cut off some of your body. No matter what pain you're in, they do everything they can to force you to stay. If you survive the pain, they give you into the keeping of someone who has complete control over you, and if you're not hated, beaten or neglected, you're brainwashed into utter helplessness.

If your body gets damaged, they don't show you how to help it fix itself; they freak out and pour poisons into it or cut out parts of it. They imprison you for at least twelve years, so that you get so used to being a prisoner that you're afraid not to be one. Then you're told you get to choose your next prison, which choice, by then, seems like freedom, but in truth you are forced to choose whatever prison has room for you, because if you don't, you won't eat.

They tantalize you with distorted possibilities until you *want* to numb yourself with illusions. If you do manage to summon some lifesaving rage or a desire to leave, you're brainwashed again. Of course by then they can't and don't trust you, so they make laws to keep you from reacting creatively to their insanity. Then they tell you that since you have this problem of not feeling loved, you should learn to love yourself, pamper yourself, turn inward and forget about how diseased and crazed everyone else is.

Some decide to fight the insanity, which just goes to show how much they've become a part of it, and some decide to love it, which just goes to show the same thing. Meanwhile, more and more ways of tightening the web of insanity are invented. The only way you manage to survive instead of succumbing is to keep believing in your vague memory of where you came from. Is there any reason for all this? Is there anyone out here with an answer?

From the perspective of the ideal, of home, the planet does appear to be the way you're describing it.

Tell me about it.

When you've come home, health is the natural state of a body that is regarded as a perfect instrument of self-maintenance. Harmonious community is the natural outcome of mutual respect and love. Everything that is needed is available in abundance. Which is why some do go back, to remind the ones who have forgotten what home feels like. They use the tools available, the instruments and languages, to write music and poetry, to tell stories, and create images. They hope that if they spark the memory, the contrast will become self-evident. The fear mongering will be seen to be as confining as it is, in comparison to living in the freedom and wholesomeness of their origin. You knew when you went, though, didn't you, little lost soul, that you could reserve yourself some fairly decent accommodations?

I didn't go to see the polished surface. I went to find out what it was really like there. Whew. Intriguing, but devastating.

Intriguing, yes, which is one of the reasons for returning. De-vast-ating, precisely. Others return to help re-vast-ate those who have forgotten who they are. Some would like to transform the whole place, but of course no one can force that to happen, they can only offer the option. So, you'd prefer not to return?

Eventually everyone gets out anyway, right?

Oh, well, eventually, yes. Some of those who go back do so because they see a life wasting in prison as a life wasting in prison, when it could be a life engaged in freedom. Those who don't go back are free to explore different places created by others, or to create their own place, to be at home without a body and do whatever they want to do.

What would happen if the insanity there got so out of hand that they destroyed the place? Not that I care. Seems like a natural outcome, a disease killing its host and itself at the same time. I mean, once they're released from prison, they're free, right?

Indeed, one of the more beautiful outcomes would be masses of released prisoners, as you call them, or travelers, all finding home at once, not because they were able to destroy the host, as you call her, since that would be up to her, but because they were tired of feeling lost within a density they did not know how to escape otherwise. This is one of the visions.

Another is the transcendence of the entire place into a living mansion of ease, and although that, too, would be one of the more beautiful outcomes, there is no attachment. There are many possible outcomes.

The hostess (shall we call her?) is like a good mother, one who will encourage exploration, tolerate mistakes, try to pre-

vent harmful actions, offer helpful guidance, and frown on abuse. If the abuse becomes insistent, she looks for the pain behind it and offers remedies. If the pain has become the only way to heal, she endures the pain until the healing demonstrates its form, which may be a change in form. Like a good mother, she never insists on imposing her wisdom or controlling an outcome for another being. She lets the wisdom of another determine itself.

That, as you know, is a universal given. That is what maintains the diversity of how freedom is used to create experience. That is why some choose not to return. They have no interest in that particular way of experiencing freedom.

Isn't that a paradoxical twist? Using one's freedom to imprison oneself and others? That's nuts.

For a timeless, dimensionless being to focus itself into the confinement of time and space is to experience paradox. The ways of focusing are infinite. The ways of inserting oneself into our present place of discussion are countless. You can go in as a curious onlooker. You can go in with an itinerary. You can go in with a plan. You can go in for the challenge. You can go in for a vacation.

Vacation? There?

Some who have been elsewhere, or even there in a different time slot, would consider themselves to be living better than kings and pharaohs, with all kinds of conveniences at their fingertips—playing games, solving mysteries, creating beautiful environments, appreciating the diverse beauty of the hostess, communicating with other species. It is not a place without wonder.

There's no place like home.

Home is where the heart is.

You have to love it or it isn't home, you mean?

What you love is home. The more you love, the bigger home is. You can make anything home by loving it.

Uh oh, now you're starting to sound like that insanity.

You don't have to love the insanity, or the pain, or the

numbness, or the cruelty. If you did, it would become home to you.

If it became home to me, I wouldn't want to change it, because I would be comfortable with it as it was?

Exactly. If you don't want to be at home with being diseased, don't love being diseased. Love health. Embrace it as your own. Envision it, project it, and experience it. If you want to be at home with freedom, love freedom, your own and everyone's. Envision it, project it, and experience it.

What I love is home.

Which is why you are floating around out here. You are loving this, and not that. You are, for the moment, choosing to be detached and separate, and not a part of the planet.

But to some that planet feels like home.

And to some, that planet is within home, not outside of it.

Oh! So, I have the freedom to experience everywhere and everything as part of the home I love.

That would be the greatest freedom, yes.

But what if I didn't want to experience ignorance as part of my home?

You don't have to choose the greatest freedom. You can choose the freedom to create a home in which you include only what you choose to love. But this is a limited freedom, which can, if one is not careful, become the need to impose a limited freedom on others.

Hmm. Those who are on the planet experiencing a limited freedom, how do they get home if they don't want to be there any more?

They can leave it, they can live it, or they can love it. They can die to what doesn't feel like home; they can re-create their experience so it feels like home, cleanse the environment of whatever they don't want in their home; or they can love it as it is and it will become home.

So when someone there says, I want to go home . . . ?

They can be at home. The body they are using as a focus in time and space can be put on hold. Or it can be released back to the hostess as reusable materials. Or it can be used to take them to where they love being.

Wow, there are a lot of possibilities I didn't consider when I was caught up in the insanity. I probably missed a lot. Not that I want to go back to find out what I missed. There are plenty of other places to explore, right?

Oh, yes. And you have all the time you want, to hop about, to delve deeper into one place, to go nowhere, to seek adventure, to return to what draws you, to avoid what doesn't. That place in some ways is a miniature version of what else there is in the universe. The maximum version actually has no limits, but some seem to like certain limits to their experience. It's all open to your choosing.

I have a lot to think about.

If thinking is what you want to do.

Now that you mention it, no, I really don't want to think any more for a while. I'd rather just float in all this peace and love and warmth and light. It's good to be home.

Meanwhile, back on the planet in question, a middle-aged woman walks out of her house into a warm blustering November night. A wind from the southwest is cascading even more leaves from the maple tree onto a patchworked carpet of yellow that glistens beneath the patio light. Below a star-dotted sky of velvety black, clouds splash and foam above the countryside. As her graying hair blows across her drizzle-moistened face, she is reminded of the gift she was given the day before. A shy woman, pushing a helpless man in a wheelchair, hesitantly handed her a book. She opened a version of the New Testament to the book-marked page.

The wind blows wherever it pleases. You hear its sound, but you cannot tell where it comes from or where it is going. So it is with everyone born of the Spirit.

She is taken up by the wind as she walks. She becomes the wind, wet and alive and stirring the trees into a whispery roar, blowing in from somewhere warm and going wherever it pleases. She hears the echo of a conversation in the vast wild sky, and she smiles about her lost soul self, and about the part of her who knows what home is. She loves the freedom of the wind. The wind is home. She loves the stars. She loves the night. She loves the light shining from the window where her partner sits at his computer, doing what he loves to do, encouraging other lost souls on the planet to awaken to the light of love, to come home.

39

Short Circuit

David's brother has been continuing to move his things into the apartment, and David has been coming home from the store to my place with reports of Angel's reactions, which have ranged from vociferous comparisons between the way she's being treated and Nazi concentration camps, to a door being slammed so hard that a glass pane fell out.

Our first customer, on the day we opened the store, was a woman I hadn't seen in years. Bernie hadn't anticipated finding me there. She'd just felt drawn to check out this new place when she and her son and her new man friend were going by. As we caught up with one another—she'd been a social worker, and now she has her own counseling practice—her nine-year-old son wandered around the store, gravitated to one of

David's walk-in pyramids, and plopped himself down underneath it. She wanted to buy one of my paintings but didn't have her checkbook with her, so would I put it aside for her? When she was ready to leave, her son, who'd in the meantime picked out a polished stone for himself, put up his hand in a gesture of wait-a-minute-Mom, and went back into the pyramid for one more long moment of whatever he was receiving inside it.

When I delivered the painting to her, we sat and talked for a while in her office, which had an energy in it I can only describe as buoyant and cushioning, the way a cloud looks like it would feel if you could lie back into it, gently supported above and away from all cares. She wanted me to know that on the day of our store's opening, her son had been distressed about her divorce situation and wasn't talking to her. She'd been at a loss about how to help him, but when she saw him go into the pyramid, she was relieved to be reminded that he was perfectly capable of finding exactly what he needed for himself. In fact, when they left, he *was* himself again, cheerful and open. So our meeting again on that day was an important turning point for her, and meant to be, she said. She was also happy to have my painting.

Yes, it was meant to be, in more ways than one, I thought later. I myself had just been reminded that there are people in the helping professions who are spiritually conscious and full of love. I called Bernie and asked her for some information. She directed me to some of the county departments that might be able to help an emotionally distressed homeless person.

I reported my findings to David. After five phone calls, I'd learned that unless Angel was suicidal or threatening others' lives, we couldn't expect any help from Crisis Intervention, but she could volunteer herself for evaluation, apply for financial assistance, and receive help finding a shelter. If she didn't agree to being helped in any of these ways, our only recourse was to call the police, and they would take it from there. She probably wouldn't end up in jail. She would most likely be diagnosed and prescribed a medication that would mute the voices she hears so she could think more clearly, and then be assisted to find a suitable living situation. I sighed. It didn't seem likely that Angel would be amenable to seeking community help, considering her deep-rooted paranoia about government surveillance. I concluded, "I can't imagine you calling the police, David, even though you're the one who would have to do it."

David was stressed. He'd started working for his friend Dan to supplement the meager income from the store; he couldn't see how he was going to pay the rent without his brother's help; and his brother wasn't getting any happier about moving in with Angel still there. He'd been working seven days a week. He needed some time to himself. The seasonal rush of art and craft shows was finally slowing down enough for me to offer to tend the store for a day to give him a break.

"Are you here alone?" Angel asked me when she sauntered into the store.

"Yes, I am," I answered, looking up from beside the woodstove, which was just starting to warm the place up.

"I heard you talking to some men in the basement."

"Nobody's here but me."

"Tell David there's something wrong with the circuit breaker."

The way in which she phrased her request made something go wrong with my circuit breaker. All my resolve to be helpful if my help was asked for and to stay out of what wasn't my business sputtered and crackled, and I blurted out, "*You* tell him. You're always telling him what's wrong! You do nothing but complain! You've never ever thanked him for keeping a roof over your head for these last eight months!"

"Now I know what the face of evil looks like," she said, narrowing her eyes at me.

"Why don't you just leave?" I yelled, totally out of control. "You keep saying you're going to leave! Why don't you just do it! Don't you get it yet? David is waiting for you to leave!"

"You look like a witch," she commented calmly.

"He can't afford to pay the rent unless his brother moves in and helps out. He can't afford to keep supporting you!"

"You are incredibly ugly," she informed me.

"Just freaking leave!"

She walked out, and if David's brother hadn't walked in five minutes later, I would have spent the better part of the day shaken, but he nodded his head when I told him what had just happened. "I had a shout-down with her myself a few days ago. It looks like it's going to come down to having to call the police."

Despite his calm assessment of the situation, I regretted my outburst. How could I have lashed out at someone who has suffered so much? How could I have let myself join the enemy of her tortured mind? She was right. I'd become an evil, ugly witch, enflamed with rage. I woke up that night kicking the covers off and needing to pray for her.

Little one. You have suffered the secret of your past for so long. You are not the guilty one. The world does not judge you. Separate the past from the present. The present is a world where you can ask for help. You need only ask. You will not be betrayed if you ask. You will not be abandoned. You will not be judged. You will not be silenced. Ask where you belong. Ask where you are needed. Ask where you can be comforted. Ask where you can be whole again, and you will be shown.

As I prayed, I saw an image of Angel looking like a saint, with a light glowing all around her and an infinitely peaceful expression on her face. I thought perhaps I was seeing her dreamer, for her eyes were closed. Yet, had she opened them and become her own awakened self, it seemed she would have viewed with love and understanding her role and ours in this unfolding drama. I found myself thanking her for whatever purpose she was serving.

"Mom," Fawni said to me the next day, "did you know there was a fire at the yellow gate?"

"What?" I'd noticed, the last time I'd gathered up the trash bag, that the rains had all but melted the Saran-wrapped paper

Welcome sign I'd taped over the Please-don't-litter sign, so I'd peeled it off, and hadn't yet gotten around to replacing it. "A fire?"

"Yeah, when I came home last night, there were all these fire trucks blocking the road."

I took a walk and checked the damage. None of the trees were charred, but all the dead leaves covering an area the size of my house were a blackened mass of ashes. Someone had probably carelessly thrown down a lit cigarette. Fortunately, the local fire company had arrived in time to avert a serious disaster.

A coincidence is nothing less than the details of our interwoven stories, the effects of our overlapping projected energies, expressing themselves. I couldn't match up the times of my outburst and my prayer with the start of the fire and its dousing, but I didn't have to. I'd been given an admonition. It's one thing to ignore the seductive pleas of a broken puppet, but it's quite another to pick it up and smash it against the wall. It's fine to walk away from a house of repetition, but it's a violation of others' free will to bulldoze it to the ground with people inside it. It's a good start to put up a Saran-wrapped sign to let the universe know you've changed your attitude, but wouldn't a wooden one say it with a wee bit more conviction?

The community, people I didn't even know, had prevented a serious disaster.

Yesterday David asked me to write down all the numbers I'd called for community help about housing and financial and emotional support. He was going to give them to Angel, give her another chance to help herself, and then, he said, if he had to, he might just talk to the police.

40

Through the Woods

Several months after my divorce was finalized, my ex showed up to tell me he'd been to the doctor. His liver was seventy-five percent dysfunctional. His brain had atrophied. He didn't know how long he had to live, so he wanted to make peace.

"I've never done this before, B.," I told him, "but lie down on the couch, and I'll try to do a healing on you."

He laid down on his stomach and fell asleep as I slowly passed my hands over his body, about six inches above it, from head to foot, twelve times. I opened my crown chakra and asked that universal energy come through me and pass into him. I felt my hands grow hot as I sensed white light sparkling with rainbows coming through me. I pulled the light into my body, into my liver, my brain, into all the parts of me that were healthy, to send a reminder of health into his body. When I was finished, I sat quietly until he woke up. "Do you feel any better?"

"I feel peaceful. I'm not angry any more. My anger's gone. You gave me that."

"You gave me a lot, too."

"I can see your aura!" He was surprised. "It's white, with rainbow colors in it!"

Three days later I was at my sister's place in Montana for a family reunion, and I noticed that my neck, which had been stiff and sore for the past two years, was okay. Hmm, that was interesting. Whoa. My toe was okay, too, I noticed, wriggling it. I'd fallen, shortly after B. had moved in, and broken my big toe and damaged the nerve in my left leg from the knee down. Wow, I could feel myself touching my leg! It wasn't numb and tingling any more! I checked the other problems I hadn't been able to heal while I was focusing on interacting with his angry, helpless energy. No more infection on my gum. How . . . ? Oh, my. Was *I* healed when I did the healing on him?

When I came home, Raine told me she'd had to insist that B., who'd decided to set up his tent in my front yard while I was gone, get off the property. He'd yelled at her that she was sick, and she'd yelled back, "*I'm* sick? *You're* sick!"

"No, I'm not," he said. "I went back to the doctor, and he said my liver's fine."

I don't know if that was true. B. said a lot of things that he wanted to be true, and a few months later he returned to ask if he could leave his body on my land. At the time, I hoped it was true, but all I knew for sure was that the rainbow-sparkled white light coming through me had healed everything my body had manifested as warning signs of clogged energy. I thanked my body for having demonstrated what I was doing to myself and for having responded so instantaneously to my intent to heal. I promised I would always listen to it from now on and re-create my intention for health and wholeness whenever it suggested that I was doing otherwise.

One of the members of our book study group invited two

people to give us a three-hour sample of the weekend seminars they'd been conducting in various countries around the world. We sat in a large circle in Brooke's living room. After an introduction, we were led into a meditation and guided to visualize ourselves entering a forest, making a medicine wheel, and meeting with the self we'd left behind.

Despite the speaker's slow, calm instructions, I found myself joyfully spiraling into somersaults, curtseying to the trees who swayed into hula dances in response, and plopping neon green jiggly-jello rocks into a circle. Trying not to laugh out loud at my vision so I wouldn't interrupt anyone else's, I stood at the edge of my medicine circle and summoned my forgotten self. And there she was, nine feet tall, a being of white light sparkling with rainbow colors. She beamed her love toward me. I slipped into her and looked back across the medicine circle at the body housing this lifetime's personality. I remembered how confining that body had felt so many times, how I'd wanted to rip it open like Clark Kent's shirt and reveal the big LB underneath, how I'd forced myself to squelch that desire, to dim my light for fear of being considered alien, insane, or too full of myself. I liked that body better now. Like an old sweat suit, it had grown saggy and comfortable. I slipped my Light Being self back into it, and walked out of the woods, over the sill, and into a clearing full of sunshiny rainbowy light.

As the other people in the room shared their tearful reunions with their long-abandoned child selves and asked how they could overcome depression and feel connected to life again, I wanted to wave a magic wand and open their eyes to the glowing soul I could see around each person. But the woman who was responding to their questions, I noticed appreciatively, was relating to each one of them exactly where they stood on their own path, somewhere between kindergarten and God, between here and perfect, learning to balance the mundane with the miraculous. She glanced at me, and mouthed a thank you to me. I returned the gleam in her eye.

Living on this planet, having chosen to be here at this time, isn't about being catapulted into heaven. It's about immersing oneself into the problem and finding a solution from the inside out, even as we witness it from the outside. It's about exploring the Mystery, playing our part, consciously dreaming our reality, experimenting with who we are, and slowly but surely drawing heaven down around us, like the gentle silent snowflakes that are drifting past my window.

41

Imagine That

The only time I was regressed into a past life by an instructor, about twenty years ago, I was so skeptical that I decided beforehand to startle her by describing an extraterrestrial past life. I became so engrossed, however, in the vision of a lifetime spent as a spherical being of light on the second moon of the planet Fa, that I found I could barely respond to what felt like annoyingly irrelevant questions.

Each being living on that moon was a ball of energy that could change colors, although one basic color was its original essence. It could merge with another being and create a sphere of another color. I was a peachy pink, and where I overlapped with a being who was pale blue, we became lavender. Each ball of energy could reduce itself to a point, or expand itself to the size of the whole moon, the surface of which was a vast expanse of colorful, glowing sand, tiny chips of crystals and gems.

At the moment of my imagined-memory-vision, the deep purple sky was crackling open, being split into shards by white lightning. The moon-planet was about to explode. The other spherical beings and I collected into groups and promised one another that we'd reappear together in another part of the universe after the explosion.

I emerged from the vision dazed and confused, and promptly dismissed it. When I shared this almost forgotten experience with David during one of our early conversations, he exclaimed, "I've seen those spherical energy beings of different colors! I didn't know why they were different colors, though. Now I understand why—they each have their own individual wavelength. I've *seen* them—and you *are* one!" He'd studied the hierarchy of etheric bodies and planes of existence, and had visited some of them. Various beings in different forms had shown him where people go when they die and where those beings that have never incarnated reside, so his unquestioned acceptance of the *reality* of my memory put it into a new light, no pun intended. Even as I write this, I'm beginning to make the connection between that memory and my family of Light Beings.

Do we have incredibly wonderful imaginations?

Does God?

Where does imagined end and real begin? Where does infinite end and finite begin? Where does eternal end and this moment begin?

Can we imagine our universe to be but an atom within a vaster universe that is merely an atom within an even vaster universe, on and on, without end? Can we imagine that every electron within this universe encompasses another universe, within which every electron encompasses another universe? Can we comprehend that the lifespan of a fruit fly is but a fraction of the lifespan of a human being, which is but a fraction of the lifespan of a God we can have conversations with, which is but a fraction of an infinite, eternal Source? Can we imagine that living parallel to this life of ours is another self living the life that broke off from our last decision, that took the left branch of the tree when we took the right?

If we can imagine, and experience as real, such voluptuously rich and extensive regions of existence, how hard can it be to imagine, and then experience as real, the perfect job waiting for us to find it, the perfect health we desire replacing this disease, or the most delicious love serving itself up as dessert to all the dishes we've tasted from the buffet of life? Can we imagine, until we do indeed experience it as real, that a Christ Consciousness resides within us, that we are the ones it was foretold would someday do all of this and more?

Last night my stepdaughter and I reviewed the perfect timings involved in her being so close to teaching at the Waldorf school. Her son Eli was not accepted a year ago when she applied for him to enter the third grade. They would have to wait for another child to leave, and there were six children on the waiting list. She figured she'd probably have to homeschool him, and toward that end, she took a summer Waldorf teacher training course, which I happened to be able to afford for her. She had prepared a semester's worth of activities when she was informed that another child had left and that they'd chosen her son from the waiting list. Wow. Okay!

Then, since she'd be driving him a half-hour to and from school, she looked for work nearby that would fit into that schedule and found an opening in the day care center affiliated with the school. Her proximity allowed her to attend the teachers' and administrators' meetings, and she became a familiar and appreciated contributor to the discussions. Only after attending the meetings for her own elucidation did she learn that one of the teachers might not be returning next year, and her very impressed trainer suggested that she apply for the position, with his recommendation.

She started this train of events wanting the best for her son, and in the process discovered what she herself would most passionately love to do. A dream she hadn't even considered a year ago is now unfolding before her eyes.

She and I finished our discussion and went downstairs into the kitchen, where we had to dodge out of the line of fire between Daniel's water pistol and Eli's plant-mister-turned-sharp-shooter. As I pulled a carton of milk from the refrigerator, it slipped from my hand and spilled onto the floor. "Bo!" I called our collie-husky. "Help! Clean this up for me!"

"You never get irritable!" my stepdaughter observed. "I wouldn't have grumbled about cleaning up the mess, either, but you take it a step further, you cheerfully give Bo a treat!"

"Oh, Raine, I'm not being cheerful," I told her as Bo industriously licked the brick floor under the boys' crossfire. "Just before you got here, I was recovering from a surprise visit."

My ex-husband, whom I haven't seen in over a year, called because he needed a copy of our divorce papers. I went outside when I heard his truck pull up on the driveway, but since he'd brought his younger daughter along, I invited them in. "So, are you getting married again?" I asked, handing him the envelope. He was indeed. "Congratulations. I'm really happy for you. And are you going to have the son you always wanted?" I probed, rather shamelessly.

"Well, almost, but, no, that's not going to happen," he said with absolutely no indication that he hadn't already dealt with the situation quite masterfully. "Are you really happy for me?"

"Yes. Yes, I am. I was just recently remembering the healing I tried to do on you, and I hoped you were well."

"I went back into rehab for two months, and I'm on medication now. I'll have to take it for the rest of my life, but that's okay. I'm working again. I brought some photos along of the addition I just built." It wasn't just the home improvements he showed me that were impressive.

His daughter, who'd hated school when we were all living together, and who's been known to go for months at a time not talking to her dad, smiled at him, and reported that she loves getting up in the mornings now, because she's spending her mornings at a day care center, working with great little kids.

When they left, the hugs that we shared were delicate, but deeply meant.

"And even though it was such a good visit, Raine," I finished my story as Eli went screaming out of range with Daniel in pursuit, "it brought up so many emotions it left me flattened." Of all the reasons why I thought I'd originally invited him into my life—my proclivity for being a sucker for helplessness needing to be reckoned with by facing and overcoming my own helplessness, my dispute with anger as a means of communication needing to be settled by my finally owned self-protective outrage, my soul rounding itself out by mirroring its exaggerated fears and secret, dark, hidden power to itself, my karma needing resolution—I'd forgotten a major one. I loved him.

I closed the door behind them and would have cried with relief and gratitude if Raine and Eli hadn't knocked and opened it again. "I didn't call Bo over to clean up this mess because I'm cheerful! I just didn't have the energy to do it myself."

Raine couldn't finish her sympathetic comment. She had to duck or get drenched.

Who would have thought that thirteen-year-old Daniel and eight-year-old Eli would take to one another like the brothers that neither only child has?

Sometimes life turns out even better than we can imagine.

42

Zap, You're IT

David accepted my birthday present with grunts and groans and seventeen reasons why he didn't want or need a weekend Level I Reiki class. Reiki-shmakey. He knows all that stuff. But the day after our attunements, when Daniel (who still has headaches even though he's being tutored at home) stayed over, David was prompted to ask Fawni and me to join him in doing a healing on his son. For twenty minutes the three of us surrounded Daniel, lying on his back on Fawni's massage table. Each of us listened to our own intuition, letting the universal light energy make use of our loving intent however was needed. That night Daniel was able to do something that he says hasn't happened in a long time. He slept. Straight through, for eleven hours. And he woke up with no migraine.

The next evening, on our way to a movie, David and Daniel went into a Walmart while I waited outside in the car. Since I had nothing better to do, I decided to zap Walmart with universal light energy. Keeping my open palms aimed outward (below the level of the window, so passersby wouldn't wonder if I was being held at gunpoint by a figment of my imagination), I beamed my intent for the blessings of the Christmas spirit to infuse itself into the entire store. As people went in and out, I gave them an extra little secret zap.

I assumed I'd have no way of knowing if I was being effective, but I was enjoying the possibility, when a man stepped through the door and lit a cigarette. He inhaled, narrowing his eyes over the smoke. He looked stressed, like he needed a break. I aimed the beams from my hands right at him, while casually looking here and there, being just some woman sitting in her car keeping the motor running. He took a last drag, threw the butt down on the concrete, twisted his shoe over it, and then started smiling as if he couldn't help himself, smiling and frowning at the same time. A peaceful expression softened the lines of his face. He glanced over at me, a question forming in his eyebrow. But my eyes didn't linger on him, even though my hands were aimed right at him through the car door. He walked around the corner smiling, while I sat in my car chirping like a two-year-old with a new bathtub toy.

A Reiki attunement is one human being passing on to another the permission to use oneself as a radio. You don't need permission, but you might need reminding—that the music is already in the air, and all you have to do is just turn your dial to, say, a choir of angels singing, and when someone nearby hears it, they remember the delicious loveliness of well-being. Universal light energy isn't just in the air, though, it's in the sidewalk, in your trousers, in the stubbed out cigarette, in the sweat on your palms, in the marrow of your bones—it's everywhere. It's so incredibly abundant we will never run out of it. We can't run out of it. It's the stuff we're made of. It's what we're using to create a foul mood or a frantic one, a fear or a folly or a fine work of art.

All we have to do is shape it with our minds, sing it into form, tune it to whatever frequency we want to, and watch the results. Someone might not want to hear a choir of angels singing, so they tune it out or walk away, and that's fine, but as long as you are enjoying listening to the crystalline harmony of joyful resplendence, why not stay tuned to that frequency—someone else might be moved to turn a corner that changes the course of his life.

What I learned during our attunements surprised me—I can actually feel, as I pass my hands slowly over someone's body, whether an area is pulling energy from my hands or resisting it. If I still myself, empty myself out, keeping only the gentle intent of being a hollow reed for the greatest wisdom, I can feel differences in temperature, density, and activity, and my hands respond, sensing and enhancing the direction of the flow.

I learned that if you send someone a dose of universal light energy and they aren't receptive to it, it will be kept on hold until they are. It's like opening an account of healing energy that can be drawn on even years later. Every minute that we spend sending healing intentions to anyone, anywhere on the planet, will be made good use of and will never be wasted.

And what else I learned from our practitioner is that you can do Reiki on anything—your VCR, your cat, your potted plant, your car. On my car? On my car's windshield wipers?

So, Master—Reiki is the same thing as laughing at myself when I'm forgetting who I AM?

Yes, Grasshoppah, *now* you can burn the dragons into your forearms.

Uh, yeah, well, that's okay; I wouldn't want to disfigure my tattoo.

43

The Path Not Traveled

When I was seventeen, in that still innocent year of 1961, I wanted to join the Peace Corps, change the entire world for the better, marry a man I'd love deeply and devotedly for the rest of our lives, and adopt children from many cultures as brothers and sisters to our own.

If anyone had told me that two years later I would give up on the Peace Corps because I'd travel around the world and be so devastatingly disillusioned by the rampant discrepancy between wealth and poverty that I'd stop believing entirely in one person's ability to make any difference at all . . . if anyone had told me that the first man I'd fall in love with would commit suicide . . . or that I'd graduate from college only to spend nine years in twelve different jobs . . . or that I would divorce the father of my son, never marry the father of my daughter, and become a step-mother to three other children . . . that I would spend two years trying to fathom the abyss into which a teenager with multiple personality disorder had fallen . . . that I would take my father to Mexico in search of something other than radiation, chemotherapy, or surgery to reverse his cancer, only to have him decide to die anyway . . . that I would eventually marry and divorce a suicidal alcoholic . . . that I wouldn't acknowledge my talent as an artist until I was nearing fifty . . . well, I probably would have thrown in the towel on the spot.

Because no one could have reassured me, after such an outline, that traveling around the world would also make me fall in love with every culture I'd have the privilege to taste and smell and touch, and would persuade me to embrace human beings as essentially and pervasively openhearted, good-natured, industrious, and eager to share. I would never have foreseen that having loved someone who didn't want to stick around would become the impetus toward piercing the veil and opening communication between the visible and invisible realms. No one could have explained to me that tossing one job for another again and again would strengthen my sense of choice, broaden my empathy for people who feel stuck, and give me such a variety of skills that I would end up being able to design, help build, and maintain my own house, which would become a welcoming haven to so many.

Nor would I have understood how many times I was going to discover that I had karma to resolve, and that the members of my Light Being family were going to be around to help me resolve it. I wouldn't have comprehended that some of the best gifts I'd ever receive were going to be stumbled upon in the valley of the shadow of death, and that sharing someone's passage to the other side would relieve me of so many imagined limitations and unnecessary grief.

Nor would I have understood that working with a broken psyche until it healed would allow me to witness the profoundly inspiring stamina and courage of the wounded, or would allow me to see every human being as a large crowd of selves waiting to discover themselves as a whole that is greater than its parts. No one could have persuaded me that giving up on someone I'd wanted to save would be the cure for both our diseases, or that having waited to acknowledge my talents until I'd finished fully sharing my children's development into self-sovereign individuals would give those talents time to simmer and mature, and would surprise the bejeebers out of me just when I thought I was way, way past being surprised.

That life is a mystery is a wonderful thing.

44

Rounding the Corner

There is really no such thing as closure. And there is.

David's once-girlfriend began asking for help, from her spiritual group, from the women's shelter, from her father, from her neighbor, and from a friend. She has moved in with two people who welcome her and need her. Both David's prayer and mine have been answered! David's brother is completing his move into the apartment. He and David are planning to give classes in healing, meditation, and yoga.

Members of my book study group have solidified plans for the spiritual center. They have materialized funding and are beginning renovations on the property.

There are no ducks left at the public lake, and many of the Canadian geese have flown as well. I don't know if we'll ever see Hewlett and Packard again, but the privilege of having dis-covered what a duck knows best will always be both the same.

I have quit smoking, because suddenly one day it was just easy. David thinks he might quit, too. We've both done so before. Will we stick to it? It doesn't seem to matter. It's not about smoking. It's about being abundantly inclusive of all of who we are, from the inside out, and then rearranging our-selves in whatever way feels best to be.

I thoroughly enjoyed having my son home for the holidays. I didn't even know how much closure I felt for Eric's child-hood until he announced that it's time to start listening for the name of the new little person he and his girlfriend Nicole are inviting into their lives. My son is going to be a father! Some bright soul has chosen to join him in the adventure of living! I'd forgotten—our whole family isn't all here yet!

I look forward to this new generation, to how much truer to themselves they have the potential to be. When my grand-mother was a child, she was not permitted to view her own body. She was bathed with her head poking through a cloth draped over the tub. She dreaded the consummation of her marriage and didn't trust her own mothering instincts. She ended her own life, a lonely and unhappy woman, when she was sixty-three. My mother, an only child, spent her adoles-cence in a boarding school, but as a mother she stayed at home with her three children, and despite her fears and limitations, imbued us all with enough hope and strength to be able to develop a trusting relationship with the universe by the time we reached maturity. At seventy-eight, she has retained almost none of her memory, but every present moment is received with the openness of a child, and she expects her afterlife to be a new adventure.

I managed, because my children demonstrated themselves to be at least my equals, to stay out of the way as they insisted on minimizing their fears, cultivating their independence, and becoming partners with the universe. I expect the rest of *this* life to be the best part of my adventure yet, even as I watch my grown children take over masterminding our family reunions into gently hilarious, openhearted, meaningful celebrations, while I fade into the background with unequaled contentment to make room for the unfolding of their colorful lives.

And my children's children? They won't have to *insist* on being themselves. They'll be encouraged to be so. They won't have to fight their way out of irrelevancy or long to belong; they'll know how and where and with whom they belong; they'll know from the start that life is a vastly intriguing and glorious gift. It has taken only five generations to break out of solitary confinement, out of the psyche's enslavement to utterly false premises, into born free and eager to play.

The little person coming into our lives, like so many being born into this time, will be regarded as already whole and perfect.

Fawni and I waved as Eric and Nicole boarded their plane, still filled with the warmth of our hugs. I was a little closed up inside, because watching them leave had been accompanied with a twinge of self-protection against missing them. I pulled up to the booth of the airport parking lot and had to open my car door to pay, because the electric window had just decided to stay closed. No matter how many times I clicked the button, there was no response. As we drove home, reviewing our New Year's celebration, I aimed some Reiki energy at the window.

"Mom, you know what's so amazing? I couldn't decide where to be on New Year's Eve . . . " Fawni enumerated her choices: in Massachusetts with her cousins and their friends, including one very attractive male person; or ten miles from home, at her best friend's place, where most of her friends in this area would collect; or at another friend's who was expecting mutual friends from the West Coast with whom she'd really love to reconnect; or at home with me and David and Eric and Nicole, and whoever else might show up, since we hadn't made any plans or specifically invited anyone but Dan.

"So, since I couldn't choose, I just said I wanted to be with everyone I love, and I didn't make any plans at all, and look what happened!" What had happened was that approximately forty people—it was hard to count, enough people to fill the entire house with laughter and conversation—showed up, from Massachusetts, from California, and from this area, as if drawn by a magnet—everyone that Fawni had wanted to be with.

As we all shared the rising excitement and counted down in unison, five, four, three, two, one, Happy New Millennium! our energy skyrocketed, exploding to merge with the immense, colorful wave of celebration circling the globe.

The closing of a decade, a century, a millennium, hasn't been merely the turning of another page on a man-made calendar, accompanied by a snicker about media paranoia. It has been a colossal milestone, a global rite of passage, and a sublime tribute to the connectedness of humanity. People all around the planet, ushering in this new era with everything from the most theatrical innovations of their cultures to the most heartfelt promises of protection to their children and their natural environment, are virtually and literally in touch with one another as never before.

"Do you notice something different?" I asked Fawni halfway home from the airport, rolling down the window—oh, good! It works!—to breathe in the unseasonably warm air. I couldn't tell if it was the light, the air, my own energy. . . .

"Yes! Just now, Mom! Something just shifted, totally."

It felt global, but it felt personal, too. I was suddenly lucid dreaming. I was not just a cross section of a twig, but the whole tree. I could feel the universal energy I am made of, everything's made of, flowing, connecting, being. I could see the countryside glowing with a golden light. I could feel spring warming the solar system.

I could hear humanity shedding an old paradigm, rephrasing reality.

My friend Mary, sharing her sense of the shift, asked how we could talk about it using the old language. When we use the word *sunrise*, we're being two-dimensional. Does the sun actually rise over the edge of a flat world? No. What word could we use that wouldn't be as cumbersome as Earth-rotating-into-sunlight to depict our three-dimensional awareness of the relationship of the sun and the Earth? Not to mention our shift into a fourth-dimensional awareness? She had a good point. But then she went on to describe her sense of the shift: It was like having spent years in a cave looking at the entrance and talking about the light, studying the light, questioning it, theorizing about it, wanting to know more about it, and then finally going Duh! and stepping out into it. No more need to talk about it. Just be in it.

Our language will be updated by our experience.

Surgery is being replaced by energy refocusing.

What's considered sensational news is taking on a new meaning.

General laws are dissolving into specific solutions.

Fear is being diminished by integrity.

You know this. You are part of it.

The changes we have witnessed in our lifetimes have been nothing short of miraculous. But then, miracles are as possible as once-mistreated dogs learning to trust and love human companions. The changes we shall witness yet—will they too be miraculous? Well, yes, of course, but then, miracles are as natural as well-fed puppies growing up into creatures full of expectant joy.

I could ask myself what the changes will be.

When I began writing this book, I didn't know, despite my unadmitted desire to do so, that I would meet a man who'd help me feel like I'd come home, or that the Light Being who invited me to further communications while I was lying under David's pyramid would turn out to be me. I didn't expect, despite my prayers for him, that my ex-husband would share with me the gift of his newly acquired pride in himself. My daughter, whose tuition for healing classes was a product of the new relationship I was developing with the universe, has begun to build the clientele she'd hoped for. I'm beginning to get the picture. Ask, and it shall be given. Please pass the butter. The baked potatoes. The broccoli. The cheese.

But not the dessert!

Because even though I could ask my future self what the changes will be, and even though, if I really wanted her to lean through time and whisper hints of what's around the corner, I don't really want her to. And it's not because I wouldn't understand that the outline will be filled in with unimaginable colors that I'll delight in giving away.

I want to round the corner by planting vines at its base and watching them soften its angle before I go on to explore. While part of me sits atop the maze wall swinging her feet and clapping her hands, because she's already discovered and crossed the threshold into what's beyond, this me has come to enjoy the intricate details of the labyrinthine paths, the clues, the treasures found and left for others, the turns and returns, the detours, the surprises. This me, the one with plenty of opinions and no answers to speak of, has come to a conclusion, a closure that isn't a closure.

That life is a mystery is the best thing about it.

Epilogue

After having received the twelve gifts and looking at them from various angles, it occurred to me that they were actually all the same gift. I could combine them all into one offering, into the thirteenth gift, which I would carry with me over the threshold, from where I'd pass it on.

As I consider what the gifts all have in common, I see that there are several names I could give to the thirteenth gift. Consciousness, I suppose, or perhaps universal truth. Love, most certainly, as every one of them has to do with loving myself, my life, others, you, Creation, the All—the infinite and eternal beingness of symphonic light. Yes, I'd like to remind you that consciousness, universal truth, and love are yours to do with what you will.

I'd also like to remind myself and you of the freedom that is ours when we recognize the dream and our multifaceted part in it, when we allow ourselves an unboundedly fluid motion among the infinite points of focus that we are.

I could offer you, as we approach the inevitable changes ahead of us . . . for on a global scale or an individual one, changes are inevitable, we *will* be transformed . . . by life or by death, by passivity or by involvement, by emptiness or by fullness—I could offer you the gift of your own power of transformation. We transform everything just by being, and when we use our memory, our capacity for joy, our ability to tap into the multiverse, we transform everything with a mastery of intention toward a mutually enhancing reality.

Then, too, I could call it mystery, and surrender it to you as whatever your own unraveling of your own present will reveal.

After all, though, I can call the thirteenth gift only that— the thirteenth gift. This book that you hold in your hands, this is the gift I'm passing along. Thank you for having helped me to do so, thank you for having accepted it, and thank you for *your* version of the greatest gift of all: Life.

About the Author

Born in California of German/Italian immigrants, Lesta Bertoia is the daughter of internationally renowned sculptor Harry Bertoia and is a talented visionary artist and woodcrafter in her own right. She received a bachelor of arts degree from UCLA. Bertoia is the mother of two children and the step-mother of three. She lives near Philadelphia, Pennsylvania, in an earth-sheltered home she helped to build.

Hampton Roads Publishing Company

. . . for the evolving human spirit

Hampton Roads Publishing Company
publishes books on a variety of subjects including
metaphysics, health, complementary medicine,
visionary fiction, and other related topics.

For a copy of our latest catalog,
call toll-free, 800-766-8009,
or send your name and address to:

Hampton Roads Publishing Company, Inc.
1125 Stoney Ridge Road
Charlottesville, VA 22902
e-mail: hrpc@hrpub.com
www.hrpub.com